UNSEEN CITY

UNSEEN CITY

THE MAJESTY OF PIGEONS,
THE DISCREET CHARM OF SNAILS
& OTHER WONDERS
OF THE URBAN WILDERNESS

NATHANAEL JOHNSON

RODALE

Mention of specific companies, organizations, or authorities in this book does not imply endorsement by the author or publisher, nor does mention of specific companies, organizations, or authorities imply that they endorse this book, its author, or the publisher. Internet addresses and telephone numbers given in this book were accurate at the time it went to press.

Rodale books may be purchased for business or promotional use or for special sales. For information, please write to: Special Markets Department, Rodale Inc., 733 Third Avenue, New York, NY 10017

Printed in the United States of America

Rodale Inc. makes every effort to use acid-free ♾, recycled paper ♲.

Chapter icon illustrations by Paige Vickers

Book design by Carol Angstadt

Library of Congress Cataloging-in-Publication Data is on file with the publisher.

ISBN 978-1-62336-385-7 hardcover

Distributed to the trade by Macmillan

2   4   6   8   10   9   7   5   3   1   hardcover

To Beth

CONTENTS

INTRODUCTION

THIS WHOLE THING GOT STARTED because my one-year-old daughter, Josephine, wouldn't stop asking me about the world around us. The book that you are holding is an outgrowth of my attempts to deal with her questions.

Back then, Josephine had vanishingly pale eyebrows and hair that had grown into stylish jags. When she smiled, her eyes turned from thoughtful to impish, her cheeks dimpled, and she exposed the top four of her six teeth. She was just tall enough to clonk her head when she stood up suddenly under a table. She was not yet clever enough to understand the problem, so she'd rise vigorously, driving her head into the particleboard. Then she would sit down, wide-eyed but stoic, shift to a slightly different position, and repeat the maneuver. The fontanel of her skull had nearly closed by that time. I'd check it periodically as we descended the hill from daycare, she riding in a front pack. Walking two fingers back from her forehead and over the rolling smoothness of her straight blond hair, which smelled like playground sand, I'd find good thick skull extending far enough back that I'd begin to think it must have closed entirely, and then, under the pad of a forefinger—an edge, a terrifying softness.

My every cell ached to protect her, but she did have a few unforgivable flaws. For one thing, she'd ask me to name everything she saw. Her favorite word by far was "that," usually uttered in a tone both interrogative and imperative. "That?" she would ask/command, extending an imperious finger. "That's a house," I would say.

"That!"—this time leaning backward in the front pack until I could see only the underside of her chin and her extended arm.

"That is the sky."

"That!"

"A tree."

"That!"

"Still a tree."

"That."

"Yet another tree."

It was one of those awful bargains you find yourself striking as a parent: *If you agree not to scream, I will allow you to suck the life out of me with this horrible and stultifying game.* And so, after a few weeks, I added a rule to complicate the game—I would give the same answer only once per outing. The second time Josephine inquired about a tree, I would have to be more specific. "Trunk," I would say, or leaves, a branch, a twig, a flower. And it was in this way that I noticed for the first time, though I'd walked by this tree hundreds of times, that it had tiny yellow flowers. The leaves were long and narrow, dark green on the top and, on the underside, nearly white, spotted with black. At the center of each cluster of leaves were tiny yellow flowers. I picked a few (a difficult task because breaking the supple green branch was like tearing a red licorice rope) and stuffed them in my pocket. Later, when I examined them, I saw that I had come away with about fifteen flowers, each one at a slightly different stage of maturity, revealing the stages of their development in my palm. A cluster's flowers started as little green balls that would split and open, the petals of each pushing outward and then opening backward until the five yellow petals had perfectly interdigitated with the five green pieces of the sheath, alternating yellow, green, yellow, green. Orangey hairs tufted in the middle, with a single transparent rod at the exact center. In the next stage of life, this rod rose, carried upward by a bulging green fruit swelling from beneath, the yellow bits now falling away, until finally what was left was a ball about the size of a pea, topped by a spike. I had never seen any of this before.

The next day I put Josephine in the carrier a little early so we could make a one-block detour to the bookstore. There, I bought a used copy of *The Trees of San Francisco*. My flowers had come, the book told me, from *Tristaniopsis laurina*. It was one of the most common street trees in the city, and the author noted (uncharitably, I thought, after my intimate examination) that its bloom was "semishowy." The name was a bit of a disappointment: I like a name that tells you something of a tree's place in the larger scheme of things. To pass a tree and simply register it as a "tree" is to never really see it—and certainly never notice the flowers. To pass a tree and simply register it as *T. laurina* isn't much better—worse if I memorized the name to inflict Latinate pedantry upon my friends. But knowing a name can also be a first step up a staircase to significance. *"Tristaniopsis,"* it turns out, indicates that the species resembles (*"-opsis"* means likeness) a shrub first identified by the French botanist Jules M. C. Tristan. *"Laurina"* came from the fact that it looked like a laurel tree. I liked this: It was the grittier, tougher Australian version of the Grecian laurel, this one woven into wreaths to crown rugby players and crocodile hunters rather than scholars and Olympians.

The flowers are supposed to emerge between April and June, yet all the trees—I had started noticing them everywhere by this point—were blooming in early November. Were the trees confused by San Francisco's Indian summer? Or did they bloom twice, once in the April warmth and then again in the second summer following August's false winter? If they bloomed twice, did that mean that, from the tree's perspective, two years had passed, with Earth perhaps tilting faster on this side of the globe, causing it to lay down two rings in its trunk each calendar year? None of the answers were in my book, nor were there any of the stories I'd wanted to learn once I began examining the flowers. For whom are these fruits produced for, and how does that relationship work? Was it love, enslavement, a con? I resolved to watch more carefully.

My sudden fascination with the lives of trees wasn't a random result of Josephine's "That" game. There was a reason I'd bought a book about trees rather than a book on garage doors or telephone poles, which my daughter inquired about just as often. As a kid, I'd known all the trees that grew around my home in the foothills of the Sierra Nevada, and this had given me access to a world otherwise invisible: When I saw a gray pine—scraggy branches, curving trunk, and dull, gray-green needles—I knew the earth beneath my feet was laced with serpentinite rock, and very little water. It meant I was at the lower, hotter edge of the Sierra's forests. I knew these trees are also called digger pines, after the local Native Americans, whom the white gold miners had dismissed as "diggers" miserably grubbing for food. The gray pines' twisting trunks, in the miners' view, were as useless for timber as the native population was for servitude, and the two therefore shared the epithet. What the whites didn't know was that the Indians weren't digging around these trees, they were snacking: The pine nuts in their cones are fat and tasty. (It is telling that the prospectors—who could much more aptly be described as diggers—chose to mock digging as a sign of baseness.)

Being able to decipher a bit of the language of trees made my life richer. It allowed me to see the world a little more sharply. It let me sense what was happening underground and catch a glimpse of history. It made me feel a little more confident, a little more at home—a little more rooted. I wanted Josephine to experience this same sense of connectedness. And so, when she pointed into the branches and I had nothing more interesting to say than "That's a tree," it pained me. Had I really joined the boring ranks of adults who could see nothing more than that?

Would I really allow myself to repeat this until Josephine was similarly dulled? And two years later, when Josephine's baby sister arrived, it doubled my imperative to squeeze meaning from each bush and tree.

When I started trying to learn about the natural world around me, I discovered that it's hard to find good guides to the natural history of urban environments. Until recently, people just haven't been as interested in urban ecosystems. The typical city's combination of trees from all over the world seems haphazard, and illegitimate: not really nature. In recent years, however, scientists have begun to see the romance in the vibrant messes humans have created. And because urban wildlife is sparsely studied, it is fertile ground for discovery. When Kevin Matteson, an ecologist from Fordham University in the Bronx, simply stopped to observe each flower as he walked through New York City, he identified 227 different species of bees. When Rob Dunn, a biologist at North Carolina State University, asked one of his grad students to look around while visiting Manhattan, the student discovered a species of ant previously unknown to science. And when Emily Hartop, an entomologist at the Natural History Museum of Los Angeles County, examined files from her own city, she found thirty new species. Though I could find dozens of lovingly compiled guidebooks on the wildlife of the Sierra Nevada, the topics of books I found on the wildlife of San Francisco all tilted toward convenience: A tree's roots and fruits were presented only in terms of their intrusiveness and messiness. If I really wanted to teach Josephine more than just names, I realized, I'd have to spend some time in the back stacks of research libraries.

I started fairly slowly, just groping around, trying to figure out where to find the information I wanted. I learned the region's trees bit by bit. As I did, I began to see variety where before I had seen uniformity. Where I had only seen eucalyptus, I began to see Australian willow, and red ironbark, and peppermint willow. I noticed that when Josephine heard birdsong, she would swivel her head, and so I began to stop and look too. At one corner we heard a bird singing with particular virtuosity, but didn't see it until an elderly man stepped from his garage to point to the top of a power pole. It was creamy gray—almost invisible against the morning fog—with white and black bars on its wings and tail.

"Mockingbird," the man said. "He comes and sings here for a couple weeks every year." The more closely we looked the more the world opened itself to us, as if to reward our attention.

A week later, when Josephine said "That?" and pointed at a *T. laurina,* I could at least tell her its name.

I stepped close to the branches. The leaves trailed against Jo's reaching hand. I pulled down a branch for inspection: There were none of the yellow flowers we had seen before. In their place were dense clusters of fat green fruit.

"Look at this, Josephine," I said. And for once, she didn't simply shout "That!" again. Instead, she grabbed the branch, fingered the little green pods, and murmured, "Whoa."

FOREWORD

What I'm Trying to Do Here

IT MAY NOT FEEL AS if you are in nature when you walk through a city, but you are: All around you is a densely interconnected web of nutrient exchange, competing interests, and cross-species communication. There's an invisible world right in front of our noses, ready for exploration. This book aims to give readers eyes to see that invisible world. To paraphrase Marcel Proust, the only real voyage of discovery consists not in seeking new landscapes, but in having new eyes.

When I started writing about the creatures that inhabit my neighborhood, I quickly found that there are simply too many of them to fit into one book. If I attempted to catalog every single one, I'd end up with a guidebook—a fat compilation of descriptions and bullet-pointed facts. And although I love guidebooks, alone, they aren't useful for beginners. They give data without context: Each bird or tree or mushroom is sectioned off on its own page, rather than connected to the others in a meaningful way. My goal was not to become a walking encyclopedia, but to find the richness and complexity in what I had previously thought were nondescript city blocks. I wasn't interested in facts per se, I was interested in living a more meaningful life. "Facts are stupid things," the nineteenth-century naturalist Louis Agassiz observed, "until brought into connection with some general law."

When I read a guidebook, I start to forget almost immediately. Most humans, I suspect, don't learn by memorizing decontextualized data. It's almost the opposite: We learn by trying to solve a problem, or working out a mystery. Once I have my first clue, the mystery comes alive, and the information begins to stick. Facts scatter like beads on the floor—a problem provides the thread that strings the facts into a meaningful order.

And so, instead of starting with the known and pouring on facts, I started with the unknown in these essays. I started with the puzzles that bewildered me, then sought the puzzle pieces that fit. Often, I found that one puzzle would merge into another. Why are my roses dying? Sure, they are infested with aphids, but maybe the real problem is the newest wave of invasive ants that have moved in and started farming the aphids. What is that bird screeching in my backyard? Sure, it's nice to identify the bird, but it's far more interesting if you know enough of its language to deduce that it's worried about the raccoon climbing its tree.

I was more interested in going deep than in going wide. So, to limit the scope of this book, I focused on just a few plants and animals: all synanthropes, the species that thrive alongside humans. The species I wrote about here are synanthropes that are so ubiquitous they've become invisible. I wanted to share that experience I had with Josephine: the transformation of a generic, uninteresting "tree" into something beautiful and compelling. I excluded the charismatic animals that venture into cities: the hawks, coyotes, turkeys, deer, and mountain lions. They are already plainly visible. I also avoided writing about the creatures that grab our attention because they horrify us—rats, bedbugs, cockroaches, and the like. Instead, I wanted to uncover the wonder of the creatures that are so common, so expected, that they have faded into the background.

I'd like readers walking past a ginkgo to experience the same sort of wonder they might feel among a grove of coast redwoods. I'd like them to eagerly seek out the scruffy weeds growing in the cracks of the sidewalk. I'd like readers to feel awe in the presence of the majestic street pigeon. Okay, maybe not awe, but at least a degree of respect tempered by a dose of realistic disgust and an appreciation for the ridiculous. When you actually live with nature day in and day out, you get to see it at its least dignified. This is a good, even necessary way of looking at nature, because it is honest. Nature is not always beautiful. It can be grotesque, it can be cruel, and it can be comical. If humans hope to achieve a more harmonious relationship with the natural world, we will have to see it in full: breathtaking, dirty, and inspiring, and annoying all at the same time. All too often we see only the good, or only the bad. If we can love nature for what it really is—not just as idealized perfection—we'll have a real chance of ending the strife between civilization and wilderness and replacing it with something like intimacy.

By focusing on urban—and suburban—wildlife in this book, I am breaking with the tradition of nature writing. According to that tradition, a man (it's almost always a man) goes alone into the wilderness. He comes in contact with a more authentic form of nature, is renewed, and waxes lyrical. Instead of doing that, I want to bring humans and nature back together, to see if I can find the experience of natural wonder without leaving civilization. It seems to me a more honest, and therefore a more pragmatic and useful, approach.

It turns out that a lot of popular nature writing is actually about humans and nature together; the humans just get censored. Thoreau downplayed the details of where he got his food and washed his clothes in *Walden,* and nature photography and documentary films routinely edit out signs of humanity to preserve the illusion of remote austerity. This tradition is so strong that when Annie Dillard wrote her famous book *Pilgrim at Tinker Creek,* she decided she had better not mention the surrounding suburban roads and houses. She worried that being a woman was already a strike against her, so she thought she should do her best to shoehorn her book to fit the other expectations of the genre. In reality, she was simply strolling around her town with her eyes open. Years later she told an interviewer: "I was fascinated because it was just a stupid little suburban neighborhood, but animals don't care. They don't care a bit. And I would always see interesting animals around."

I believe we can stop pretending now. It's time to give up the pretense that you have to leave home to truly experience nature, that you can find nature only in those untouched places where you can go for days without meeting people.

This, instead, is a book of domestic nature writing. Its ultimate purpose is to endow readers with a sense of belonging among their nonhuman neighbors. This kind of belonging could help tether people to the outside world. There's a measure of rootlessness to modern life. We move a lot, which means we have less time to learn local history, we no longer walk through surroundings saturated with memories. We have traded local knowledge for mobility. This lack of local knowledge yields a world that is less meaningful—literally less filled with meaning—which abrades the soul. If you don't know where you are, you don't know *who* you are, as Wendell Berry has phrased it. But meaning is all around, in the urban wildlife, simply waiting for those with the eyes to see it.

If people start paying attention to the organisms that are thriving, unseen, among us, I think it will change us for the better: On the political scale, we'll become more realistic and effective in our efforts to protect the environment; on the personal scale, we'll be happier and more full of wonder.

Cities are engineered to serve humans efficiently, usually without much regard to the needs of other species, which is why I find such hope in this fecundity, this second wave of life bubbling up, and indeed thriving, in the places we sought to reduce to purely human utility. Nature has already adapted to us; it's time we adapted to it, or at least took notice. The creatures of the unseen city could be our salve, or even our salvation.

SOME PRACTICAL RECOMMENDATIONS FOR NEIGHBORHOOD NATURALISTS

MY SOMEWHAT SELF-DEFEATING GOAL FOR this book is to inspire readers to set it down and ramble off through their backyards or neighborhoods in search of the phenomena I describe. The natural world is, for my money, the best book. But without some instruction, it's hard to read that book. I aim to provide enough of that instruction to get you started. I hope it's compelling enough to get you out the door, and to call you back out again later.

To start, here are a few practical tips that would have been useful when I started trying to learn about my own habitat.

EQUIPMENT

You don't have to buy *anything:* There are plenty of marketers out there who would like to use your impulse toward nature to separate you from your money. You don't need most of what they're selling, and the rest can be borrowed. That said, I found it worthwhile to buy the following tools. They can be truly useful for gaining entrance to the invisible city around you.

Hand lens—I love having a little hand lens (also called a jeweler's loupe) that's small enough to attach to my key ring and powerful enough to let me peer into the Lilliputian realm. A lens that provides tenfold magnification is perfect; anything more powerful becomes difficult to use. The good ones, called triplets, have three lenses to minimize distortion. Mine is a sturdy nickel-plated nugget made by Bausch and Lomb. It cost $35. It is great. I've found that a three-year old can learn to use a hand lens quite well, but a big, traditional Sherlock Holmes–style magnifying glass with a larger field of view may be more exiting for small children.

Binoculars—If you want to look closely at birds and identify them, you are going to need binoculars. There seems to be no upper limit on the amount of money you can spend on binoculars, and spotting scopes are even worse. You can get a pair of binoculars with ridiculously powerful lenses, a built-in camera, and all sorts of other rubbish. Don't buy that stuff, at least not at first. In fact, don't buy anything at all if you can avoid it: All over the world, binoculars are gathering dust in attics alongside elliptical machines, yearning for someone to put them to use. If I had the chance to do it over, I'd start by asking my family and friends if anyone had a pair I could borrow.

You'll see a number, like "6×32," describing each pair of binoculars. The first number refers to the magnification, the second to the lenses' diameters. I wouldn't buy anything over eightfold magnification because I don't have a particularly steady hand, and the field of view gets smaller and is more affected by shaking as the magnification increases. As for lens diameter, the second number, the bigger, the better. But don't get lost in the numbers: You just need something that works. If you find you are using them every day, you can always go back and get that $2,000 pair.

Guidebooks—If you want to identify the species in your neighborhood, you might start by getting yourself a guidebook to your region's trees, birds, or beetles—or all of the above, along with guides to the local mosses, lichens, and fungi. I have never regretted buying a guidebook. I find myself pulling them off my shelves far more often than any other volumes in my library. Today, anything you can find in a guidebook you can also find online. But it's a lot easier to get lost online. Unlike the vast, borderless Internet, the contents of books are usually limited to a geographic area, and that's incredibly helpful for species identification. If I find myself in the same room with an interesting-looking guide for my bioregion, I'll do whatever I can—within the bounds of decency—to take it home with me. Libraries often offer a good selection of local guidebooks.

EXERCISES FOR SHARPENING AWARENESS

Keep a journal—It doesn't need to be fancy; any set of blank pages will work. But if you're like me and appreciate a little drama in your writing tools, grab one of those black-and-white lab notebooks, or something beautiful from your local bookstore. Mine has a black cover and creamy pages. I use it to write down species names that I'd otherwise forget, along with other facts that weave these species—and myself—into my understanding of the ecosystem. I tape to its pages frivolously shaped seeds and pressed flowers. I sketch little maps of territories my front-yard songbirds have claimed. I note the dates when flowers burst, dry up, go to seed, and are eaten by birds in migration. By building this kind of record, I began to observe shifts in the seasonal patterns and to discern the otherwise invisible relationships between species. In addition to pasting actual seeds in my journal, I also record the seeds of ideas and passing curiosities. What are those tiny holes in the acorns? Why is my backyard squirrel so fat this year? How did this seashell get here, and why are shells often a rosy pink inside? When idle questions find a spot to stick and germinate, they can grow into full-fledged mysteries.

Find one rampant weed you love (to eat)—There's something about plucking a few leaves to garnish a dinner or chew as I walk that reframes my sense of my place in the warp and weft of interspecies relationships around me. There is no form of perception that we use less in understanding and experiencing nature than the sense of taste, and I find that tasting my surroundings triggers my other senses in new ways. The smell of a pepper tree is utterly novel when I grind a peppercorn between my molars and its complex fragrance wafts upward from the back of my palate to enter my nasal passages. When I'm about to eat something, my vision sharpens as I scan for signs of danger. I become cognizant of insect damage, or symptoms of disease: potential vectors of toxins, which could harm an eater, or make the eating less pleasant.

Select as your favorite a plant that is irrepressibly abundant (which is to say, a weed) rather than a species that your predations will jeopardize. Maybe it's a bitter green like dock or nasturtium or chicory that you can use on sandwiches or to garnish meat dishes. Maybe it's something sweet, like fennel. Maybe it's a flavor staple, like the nodding onion. Maybe it's the plum tree that covered the sidewalk with a sticky mess until you began collecting the fruit to make preserves.

Connect with other people—It becomes much easier to learn about your environment if you have knowledgeable people who can help you answer your questions. And there's surely an organization of naturalists near you. Every city has a group of birders. It's a bit harder to find slime-mold enthusiasts or snail clubs, but there are groups made up of people simply interested in nature in general. In the San Francisco Bay Area there's a wonderful group called Nerds for Nature that organizes species identification field trips.

You can also volunteer at your local museum of natural history. These institutions often make use of volunteers as docents or behind-the-scenes workers. You can sort dinosaur fossils at the Smithsonian's National Museum of Natural History in Washington, DC, or catalog butterflies at the Field Museum in Chicago, or put on scuba gear and clean the aquariums at the California Academy of Sciences in San Francisco. The University of California's Museum of Vertebrate Zoology in Berkeley uses volunteers to prepare specimens for its collection, which basically means skinning road-killed animals. This is obviously gross, and therefore not for everyone, but it also allows you to sit side by side with incredibly smart people and chat as you look closely at the anatomy of animals.

Finally, there are a proliferating number of citizen science projects, which won't necessarily allow you to meet people in the flesh, but will allow you to participate in real science from afar. I like YourWildLife.org, or just search the Internet for "citizen science."

Identify one new species a month—Go out your front door and, unless you are an experienced naturalist, you'll see an overwhelming number of species that you don't know. What are those grasses in the median strip, those plants in the neighbors' yard, those hovering flies? Don't try to do it all; just pick one thing that stands out and make it your mission to learn about it. Maybe it's a flower you like, or the spiders you are suddenly seeing everywhere, or the bird that wakes you up in the morning. The point is to move from perception followed by dismissal, to perception followed by curiosity. I find that simply noticing that I've noticed something (*Hey, I heard that same bird yesterday*) makes me feel good. And finding clues that suck me deeper into a mystery (*Aha, that's the bird—it's a house finch! What is he singing about?*) is even more rewarding.

I like setting a goal of one a month because it prods me to make an effort, but in a leisurely fashion. It gives me time to dig in. The point—by my reckoning—is not to become an expert in species names, but to cultivate the habit of noticing.

TIPS FOR IDENTIFYING SPECIES

When I'm starting from a place of total ignorance, I begin with a simple Web search: "Identifying X," where X is "trees" or "snails" or "spiders." Be as specific as possible; searching for "Identifying crickets" helps you zero in on an answer a lot better than "Identifying bugs" does. I look for Web sites run by research institutions, like universities or museums. Sometimes it helps to search by the scientific name to weed out the dumber Web sites. For example, I might search for "beetles" and learn that they are in the taxonomic order of Coleoptera, and then search for "Coleoptera identification." Then I might add in a few variations on my location (North America, California, San Francisco) to narrow the search. Don't expect to figure it out immediately—the journey is more important than the destination. As I make my way through this hypothetical beetle search, I'm learning: I figured out the Latinate name, and began to understand their family tree. And when I added the name of my city to the search, it turned up the Web sites of beetle enthusiasts near me. These local experts may turn out to be my best bets. I'm always able to learn much more if I have a human mentor who can show me when I'm venturing down a false path. You can also do this online; iNaturalist, for instance, is an app that allows you to submit photos to a community of enthusiasts (many of them true experts) for identification.

Another tactic is to add the term "dichotomous key" to the search. I talk about dichotomous keys in the ant chapter; basically, they are tools for identifying species that present a series of questions of increasing specificity. There are lots of them online. Find one that's simple to use and specific to your location and you'll be all set. But you should know that some of these dichotomous keys assume you already possess a lot of scientific knowledge. For instance, when mushrooms began pushing up all around my house after a rain, I made them my next identification challenge. I found a wonderfully thorough dichotomous key that was almost entirely incomprehensible to me. One part of the key asks if the "basidiocarps" are "resupinate" or "pileate, sessile." You can look up each of those words, but it takes some serious work. "Basidiocarp" more or less means mushroom. "Resupinate" basically means upside-down, so the fungal spores must come out from the mushroom's top. "Pileate" means that it has an umbrella-like cap, and "sessile" means that it's without a stalk. So, in English, this is asking: Is your mushroom growing flat across the wood, or does it have a cap that's growing out of the wood, but no stalk?

Eventually I found a guide for laymen, and that was terrific. It told me to break off a cap and leave it on a piece of paper overnight. The next morning, when I picked up the cap, it left behind a print—an intricate tracing of its gilled underside in yellowish-brown spores—as if I had run the mushroom through a copy machine. The color of the spores and the fact that it smelled like a radish helped me determine that this was an inedible poison pie mushroom.

As you do this Web searching, you'll come across guidebooks. As I mentioned, when I find something geared toward my region that looks like it would be useful, I try to get it.

HAVE FUN

None of this provides the immediate pleasure of, say, eating chocolate. It takes a little work to see the unseen. But it also doesn't need to be akin to a religious pursuit: It doesn't require years of meditation and discipline to scratch the surface. It's really not *that* hard: You should be able to find gratification after a few hours of study. If you find that you love trees, but can't get into birds, there's no shame in that. Follow your joy.

PIGEON

DISGUST COMPELLED ME TO PIGEONS. For most of my life I hadn't thought much about the birds. They were always there, invisible in their omnipresence. I suppose I must have regarded them with curiosity at some point in my childhood, but there's something fundamentally uninteresting about pigeons, perhaps by design. It's almost as if they evolved a form of camouflage that helps humans accept their presence. This isn't a camouflage against sight—they are plainly visible and not the least bit furtive—it's a kind of psychological camouflage, like a Jedi mind trick. Their bearing tells humans that these aren't the birds we're looking for, that they are not a threat, not indicative of anything in particular, but instead are unremarkable, as easily forgotten as the air, everywhere and unseen.

It makes some sense, then, that I started thinking about pigeons only once I had been shat upon. This, I would learn, is a common initiation (a baptism of sorts) into pigeon research. I found one writer after another who reported having begun paying attention to the birds after a—presumably learned, scholarly—pigeon anointed them from above.

1

The pigeon that elected me was an Argentinian pigeon. I was spending a few months in Buenos Aires, where pigeons are everywhere. Another thing they have everywhere in Buenos Aires is a type of cookie, the *alfajor*, made with the whitest of flours and *dulce de leche* (which is basically caramel, cubed). I ate one made with chocolate *dulce de leche* one evening as I was hurrying to a friend's apartment for dinner. I was brushing the last crumbs off my fingers as I trotted down the subway stairs. It was dusk, so I didn't see the white and brown globule on my sweater until I walked under the subway lights. It was about the size of my fingernail—a cookie crumb, right? *Oh no, Nate. No. Not right.*

Without thinking, I scooped up what in reality was a pigeon turd and popped it in my mouth. I spent the next several minutes on the platform flinging my hands in the air, spitting onto the tracks, turning in tight circles, and silently screaming. The other riders waiting must have wondered what they were witnessing.

Perhaps it was just coincidence, but a few hours later I grew ill. The nausea hit me just as my host served the second course—awkward timing. I reclined on the floor, broke into a cold sweat, and then settled in for a serious fever.

After that, things weren't so cool between the pigeons and me for a while. In fact, it's only recently, as I've begun to understand their capacities (beyond spreading filth), that I've gained respect for them. In the beginning, my interest in pigeons sprang purely from loathing and a potent desire to maintain distance between us. When they flew too close, I thrashed spastically at the air. I yelled and kicked at the ones that came begging near my feet. My eye sought signs of mange and disease to confirm that these were utterly revolting beasts. As I watched them, however, I also began to notice things. I noticed, for instance, that as many as half the birds in some flocks had only one good leg. They hopped around, many holding a leg gingerly off the ground. Sometimes the leg ended in a misshapen bulb. It was totally gross, but also interesting: Disgust led me to observe pigeons closely for the first time, and I then noticed something I had previously been blind to. Of course, it was something that validated my revulsion, but it also drew me in. What the heck, I wanted to know, was wrong with pigeon feet?

I should pause to say a word about disgust, because, before gathering the information that eventually endeared pigeons to me, I spent a lot of time accumulating evidence that affirmed my fears—in other words, what you learn here is going to get worse before it gets better. But it does get better. The more time people spend studying pigeons, it seems, the fonder they grow of them. For instance, here's what two of the foremost pigeon researchers, Richard Johnston and Marián Janiga, write in their book *Feral Pigeons:*

> Our chief concern in the pages to follow is to describe and analyze the biology of the feral pigeon, which we consider to be one of the masterpieces of nature. Some readers will wonder at the idea of "masterpiece" being applied to what they think of as a pest, but we hope they ultimately will join us in our opinion.

I haven't gotten all the way to "masterpiece," but what I learned about pigeons turned my revulsion into curiosity, and then, gradually, admiration. Disgust is not such a bad place to begin an inquiry. It's a good, honest emotion. It's one of those primitive reactions that simply calls a threat into focus— *Heads up, you've been shat upon by yonder fleabag.* If my interest instead began with awe, then I'd be in real trouble, because the thing that prompted me to begin digging up information would also prompt me to ignore or distort any unpleasantness I might find.

I wasn't the only one who had noticed the gross pigeon feet. A Seattle weekly newspaper, *The Stranger,* ran an article on the subject, but the experts the writer consulted had contradictory theories. One blamed predators—cats and falcons—but what predator is going to be sated by a toe? Why do they so consistently injure pigeons' feet? Another suggested that the problem was infection (with staphylococcus, perhaps). Maybe, but then, why are pigeons more commonly infected than sparrows? Another theory: Hair and string get knotted around pigeons' feet, and they have no way to untangle themselves. Again, why don't we see the same problem with other city birds? The mystery was unsolved, as far as I was concerned.

I spent my next few days in dusty library stacks looking for information about pigeon feet. As I paged through these books, I found a lot of fascinating stuff I hadn't been looking for. It was a revelation, for example, to read the simple description of a pigeon's appearance, because it made it clear that I'd actually never seen the birds—not really, in any meaningful way. If you'd have asked me to describe them, I couldn't have told you much more than: gray and gross. But reading the descriptions in these books was like seeing the grubby neighbor girl in a designer gown at the Oscars. I glimpsed them anew, dressed up in formal prose. The rock pigeon is not just gray, but "dove gray," "with deep purple iridescence at the neck that varies with the angle of the light," a "bold black median bar," and "axillaries and underwing coverts of brilliant white."

This is a description of a thing of noble beauty, the sort of creature you might find on a family crest, a bird to inspire religious metaphors. And in fact it has: For most of history there was no distinction between (scruffy) pigeons and (iconic) doves. That bird that brought Noah, while on the ark, the first sign of dry land? If you go back to the Hebrew, the word for that bird actually translates to "of the pigeon type." But at some point people began thinking of doves and pigeons differently. They are all in the same family—it's just that somewhere along the line certain species arbitrarily acquired the common name "dove," while others got called "pigeon." Some got both: *Columba palumbus* has been called both a "ring dove" and a "wood pigeon." In her book *Superdove*, Courtney Humphries suggests that it was Shakespeare that solidified the division between pigeons and doves. In Shakespeare's work, pigeons always play a functional role, while the parts for doves are consistently symbolic. The dove is "equated with peace, modesty, patience, love and other noble ideals." The pigeon usually just shows up on a dinner plate. The dove is metaphoric, the pigeon is mundane. And this division has stuck, Humphries writes: "We never talk of pigeons of peace or dove droppings on statues. 'Dove' is a pleasant enough title to grace chocolate bars and soap, while 'pigeon' has no marketing appeal." Imagine if John the Baptist had said he saw the Holy Spirit descending to Jesus "like a pigeon."

But if you are interested in getting past the marketing appeal, past the flash and dazzle of meanings we've imposed upon nature, and instead simply seeing *nature,* the pigeon is a great place to start. Has any other creature lived so closely with us, while so successfully avoiding the romantic varnish of human imagination?

As I read on, still seeking the solution to the mystery of the ugly feet but pleasantly diverted, I saw what I always see when confronted with the reality of the living world: Unvarnished nature is far more wondrous than our romantic artifice.

FAMILY VALUES

If you start watching pigeons, one of the first things you'll notice is that you never see a chick. Like some mythical beast, these birds reveal themselves to humans only after reaching maturity. There are two good reasons for this: First, pigeons are good at hiding their nests; and second, the young birds— called squabs—stay in the nest until they lose the obvious indicators of youth.

They are able to do this because mother and father pigeon work together to provide for their young. This equality in parenting extends to milk production: Both males and females secrete a cheesy yellow milk into the crop, a food-storage pouch partway down the throat. I had thought that milk belonged exclusively to mammals; it's our defining characteristic, so important that we are named for it—"mammal" comes from the

Latin *mamma,* meaning breast. Pigeons are more closely related to dinosaurs than mammals. Like breast milk, pigeon milk contains antibodies and immune-system regulators. Like breast milk, it is stimulated by the hormone prolactin; in fact, scientists discovered prolactin while studying pigeons. Despite the similarities, mammal milk isn't a relative of pigeon milk. Instead, it is an example of convergent evolution: a strikingly similar trait that arose independently in different branches of the tree of life.

As milk scientist Katie Hinde has written on her blog, *Mammels Suck*: "The production of milk independently arose after the divergence of avian and mammalian lineages over 300 million years ago. However, these milks seemingly serve the same function: body-nourishing, bacteria-inoculating, immune-programming substances produced by parents specifically to support offspring development."

Milk, in other words, is so useful that evolution created it twice.

Pigeon milk has much more protein, and much less sugar and fat, than human milk. On this diet, young pigeons often double their weight in a single day. The squabs stick their heads into their parents' mouths, thrust vigorously, and suck up a regurgitated meal. They do this for two months, after which they are relatively mature. Many other bird species leave the nest after just two or three weeks.

There are a few characteristics that distinguish a juvenile pigeon. You can look for an oversized beak—it takes them a while to grow into it—or for a pinkish-gray blob of skin where the beak meets the head; this cere turns white as they mature. But the most salient clue is the color of the eyes: Juveniles have brown eyes, whereas adult pigeons have shockingly bright, reddish-orange eyes, another of those extraordinary details I'd never noticed until I started looking for it.

The other reason you're unlikely to see young pigeons is that the nests are hidden. Pigeons were originally cliff-dwelling birds, seeking out caves in rock faces. In cities, they do much the same: The perfect pigeon-nesting location might be an abandoned apartment halfway up an old building, or a new one; workers often find pigeon nests in partially completed towers. They like to squeeze into cavelike sanctuaries protected from the weather and predators, with a flat floor to keep eggs from rolling away.

Though pigeons masterfully hide their homes, they are terrible at building them. Often, a nest consists of no more than a few twigs haphazardly arranged on a flat surface. "Most pigeons surely do not qualify as master architects," Johnston wrote. Unlike the birds that do qualify for this title—the swallows and Baya weavers, which suspend their nests from undersurfaces—pigeons that nest on narrow ledges sometimes send eggs plummeting to the pavement below.

Pigeon nests build up over time, because the birds return to the same spot. With each laying, the parents add a few twigs, but the bulk of each nest seems to consist mostly of the birds themselves. And this, if crop milk hasn't already induced nausea, is where it gets gross. The young back up to the edge of the nest and poop off the side, building up a rim of guano. A healthy pair of pigeons can lay six times a year—two eggs each time—and after few years, all those pooping pigeons can solidify a nest into a heavy plinth. Johnston found one nest that weighed four and a half pounds and contained several crushed eggs and two "mummified young." He characterized such structures as "monumental in size and longevity." We humans have the pyramids, the Arc de Triomphe, and Mount Rushmore; pigeons have piles of sticks and dead babies encased in poop. These pigeon monuments may harbor mite and insect populations, but also discourage the worst ectoparasites, like fleas, Johnston wrote. My notes on Johnston's nest findings end with an editorial annotation: "glahaahg."

AN EXPEDITION TO PIGEON HABITAT

It's counterintuitive, but the more repellant tidbits I gathered about pigeons, the more closely I wanted to look. For one thing, I wanted to examine their feet. I'd found so little on mangled feet in the scientific literature that I began to wonder if I was exaggerating the problem. I also wanted to inspect the birds afresh, so that I might see the colors and patterns and behaviors that I had been so astonished to discover. And so, on an Easter Sunday, while many kids were dyeing eggs and eating chocolate, I took my two-year-old daughter on a pigeon expedition. When I had told my plan to my wife, Beth, she blanched. Where exactly, she wanted to know, did I plan on going? "Will you please be sure to keep our daughter away from human feces and needles?" she asked.

It was a reasonable request: Pigeons prefer dense urban settings, and they congregate in open spaces. It's exactly the same environment favored by the mentally ill, drug addicts, and homeless people. I suspect that some of the disgust we feel for pigeons is associative. We've grafted our feelings about human outcasts onto these birds because they share the same spaces and hang around waiting for handouts. Perhaps we'd feel differently about pigeons if we were better at dealing with our own species.

Josephine, however, was delighted to be setting out on the expedition. As we waited for the morning train, I plumbed her knowledge of pigeons.

They are, she told me, "white."

Okay, any other colors? "Black."

"What do they do?"

"Fly." She demonstrated, one pudgy hand flapping a diagonal line from her chest to over her head. That pretty much exhausted her comprehension.

When we emerged at the San Francisco Embarcadero, Josephine got out of her stroller and ran the blocks to the waterfront, past the street artists and knickknack sellers setting up their booths. She'd promised to alert me when she saw her first bird, but she toddled past one bobbing along the concrete, and then another. Finally I knelt and wrapped an arm around her to halt her momentum. Still, she looked past the birds. I extended one arm at her eye level and pointed them out: two healthy-looking creatures strutting between an empty coffee cup and a sheet of newspaper. She drew in a breath, as if we'd spotted a condor.

"What do you see?" I asked, alert for her first, unsullied impressions.

"Pigeons" was her less-than-satisfactory response. What did I expect from a two-year-old? An inspiring quote? An original biological observation? She leaned against my restraining arm, her warm body straining toward movement.

I made one last stab: "What colors?"

"Black and white," she said matter-of-factly, then added, "and green."

And there it was: The iridescence of their neck feathers shone green on top, and purple on the undersides of their necks. I'd never registered the greenness of pigeons, and interestingly, none of the formal descriptions I'd read had noted it either. And yet Jo, in her first few seconds of work as a young naturalist, had made this discovery effortlessly. Of course, she wasn't the first; when I went back to the library I found other descriptions that did mention green. The material of the neck feathers works as a crude mirror, and tiny barbs align in such a way as to cast shimmering light that shifts with movement. Pigeon necks look even more fabulous to pigeons: They see in a broader spectrum of light than people, so in addition to the colors we perceive, pigeons see two additional colors in the ultraviolet wavelengths that we, poor limited beings that we are, will never comprehend.

When Josephine said pigeons were black and white, I assumed she meant black and a color much lighter than black whose name she had forgotten (i.e., gray). But some of the pigeons in the plaza that morning were also splashed with white. When white "doves" are released—such as at a wedding or a grand opening—they are almost always actually king pigeons, a breed with white plumage. These white birds find their way into feral groups, splattering white paint on feathers across the clan for generations.

Beyond iridescence, pigeons have just three feather pigments: black, white, and rusty brown. These are combined in three main wing patterns: bar, which is the classic pigeon look, with an armband on each wing; spread, which is essentially all black; and check, in which black and white form a crazy quilt on the wings. Much more rare are the reds, which are really a hue of light brown. These mix together in infinite combinations.

The Importance of Absurd Pigeons

Pigeon colors are important because the human fascination with the genetic determinants of pigeon plumage underpins the entirety of modern biology. It wouldn't be too much of a stretch to say that pigeons are responsible for our understanding of evolution—the master theory that governs the modern understanding of life.

Breeders have refined pigeon genetics to preposterous extremes. In her pigeon book, Humphries dreamed up instructions for visualizing some of these fancy show breeds: "Pouter: Squeeze the pigeon from its lower half like toothpaste, until its body is skinny and its breast puffs up. Then pull its legs until they are twice as long as normal pigeon legs. Stand upright. . . . Fantail: Affix a large turkey tail to the back of a pigeon. Because the tail will be too heavy, give the bird an enormous breast to compensate and move its head onto its back." Another breed, Modenas, are, according to her whimsy, "voluptuous bird pillows."

The point is that humans have figured out how to mold this species into just about anything. The genetic rules that govern pigeons are complex, but pigeon breeders developed folk knowledge that comprehended recessive characteristics, sex-linked attributes, trait suppression, and other principles long before the time of Gregor Mendel or Charles Darwin. Much of Darwin's theory of evolution, in fact, comes from observing the techniques of pigeon breeders. Most of the first chapter of *On the Origin of Species* is about pigeons. His editor actually suggested he chuck the rest and focus on the birds: "Everyone is interested in pigeons," he told Darwin. It makes a better Hollywood story to say that Darwin's revelations came as epiphanies in strange lands, but he really made most of his discoveries at home. On the *Beagle* he made some acute observations of finches, but it wasn't until Darwin made a close examination of the utterly unexotic pigeons of England that he was able to articulate a detailed mechanism explaining how evolution worked. In a very real way, the folk knowledge of pigeon fanciers is the foundation of our understanding of biology.

How High-Class Birds Became Low-Class Sky Rats

Josephine zigzagged through Justin Herman Plaza honing her curb-walking skills and pointing occasionally to a pigeon. I chased after her, bouncing the stroller down steps, then back up again when she circled around. A beautifully ugly fountain—a knot of ragged concrete pipes that are almost always dry—dominates the plaza. Unshaven, smudge-faced men napped on the grass. It's stark, but it's surrounded on all sides by postcard-perfect scenery. Along the street stand rows of palm trees, interrupted by the clock tower of the San Francisco Ferry Building. Beyond lies the bay, and on that day dozens of white sailboats ironed the water's chop. Justin Herman Plaza is a working-class retort (or un-working-class, more properly) to the upper-class waterfront. And of course, that makes it pigeon habitat. Perhaps a dozen loafed atop the pockmarked fountain.

There are people who love pigeons for their association with the downtrodden. The rapper Vast Aire, who casts himself as a pigeon in one of his songs, explained the affinity: "They are at the bottom of the food chain, but they still survive, they still make it."

Many of the people who regularly feed and cultivate relationships with pigeons are themselves on the fringes of society. They are disconnected from other people due to poverty, limited language skills, or mental illness, but they form deep emotional connections with the birds.

Before pigeons were symbols of poverty, they were gentrified. They were spread around the world by aristocrats. Before we started designing architectural features to repel pigeons, the upper class built nesting places in their houses to invite them in. The French colonial governor of Quebec, Samuel de Champlain, brought pigeons to the New World and had the workmen include a roost in his home. Every city pigeon now scrounging for crumbs is a descendant of these birds cultivated by the gentry.

How does one fall from a position as a symbol of affluence to a symbol of indigence? I suspect that the pigeon's status is inversely related to its biological success. That is, pigeons could not very well serve as a marker of nobility once they became, well, common. Aristocracy demands exclusivity.

If there weren't such an abundance of wild pigeons, they might have maintained their social position, because no one was ever able to truly industrialize pigeon farming. Unlike the mass-production-ready chicken, pigeons spend a lot of time nurturing their offspring—the parents nurse the young squabs for three months. That's why pigeons on the plate retained their exclusivity: They never became a commoner's meal.

As Europeans spread across North America they left behind a trail of pigeons. By putting up statues and courthouses and laying out public plazas, they created the habitat pigeons needed to multiply. When it became commonplace, the species turned into a humble bird of the people.

We're left with an incoherent double standard: We despise the bird in its impoverished feral state, but savor it on the menu. Most restaurateurs do their best to help us keep these two versions of the bird separate. However, there is one upscale poultry shop in Amsterdam called Pieter van Meel Groothandel in Wild en Gevogelte that makes pâté from the wild pigeons of the city. One of the shop's owners, Thomas van Meel, confirmed via e-mail that he makes "game pâté" from urban pigeons, but only after screening the birds for disease. Imagine a world in which we saw pigeons not as objects of disgust, but as a sustainable local food source.

Close Encounters of the Bird Kind

As pigeons were making their descent from bird of the aristocracy to bird of poverty, the native American passenger pigeon was going extinct. The paved habitat that allowed pigeons to spread was replacing the forest habitat that had supported passenger pigeons. We traded a bird of the trees for a bird of the city.

Feral pigeons truly are the people's bird in that they depend on us, and in a sense, they belong to us. Humans are an essential element in most ecosystems that support pigeons. There are a few wild places, like the coastal cliffs of Sardinia, where populations of pigeons remain, but even those birds forage for seeds from farms. In places abandoned by humans, like the Scottish island of St. Kilda, the pigeons have gone extinct. To idealistic naturalists of the old school, who only value nature when the human touch is undetectable, this dependency makes pigeons uninteresting at best. The original pigeon sin is that they allied themselves with humans as we tried to improve upon Eden. They thrive in our litter-strewn wake. We see our own scrappy, invasive nature reflected in pigeons, and it horrifies us.

Or maybe not. There's a simpler way to explain the revulsion pigeons provoke than claiming we see our reflection in their beady red eyes. Maybe what really horrifies us about pigeons is that they truly can be fecking disgusting.

In Justin Herman Plaza, after I'd worked up a sweat running around pushing the stroller, I lured Josephine into semistillness by offering to let her feed the pigeons.

"Want to give them some bread?" I asked.

"Huh," was her affirmative grunt.

A pair of pigeons had landed on the grass nearby and they bobbed forward, murmuring. Josephine took two slices of bread from me and hurled both overhand at the birds. Immediately, there were wings everywhere around us. At least ten pigeons fought for the scraps. A big seagull landed and swallowed the remaining crust whole. Three more seagulls appeared. Other pigeons came fluttering down. I felt my old phobia twinging as the birds edged closer, eyeing us, I thought, remorselessly.

There's something about swarming that stimulates horror deep within the subterranean unconscious. Alfred Hitchcock understood that this horror was universal enough to fuel *The Birds* with primal potency. When pigeons proliferate, they also cause more obvious, surface-level problems. An adult pigeon splatters out more than twenty-five pounds of feces a year. Fungi, such as aspergillus, feed on those white stains, and in the process generate acids that eat into statues and other stonework. The damages add up to more than a billion dollars a year in the United States alone, according to one estimate. It's likely that we spend even more than that on the pigeon-control industry, which installs spikes, netting, and tiny electric fences on buildings.

Daniel Haag-Wackernagel, a biologist at the University of Basel, Switzerland, is the probably the foremost expert on urban pigeons, and he says that none of this amounts to a real solution. Pigeons will endure shocks, fight their way through nets, and mutilate themselves on spikes to get to their homes. "No repellent system we tested can keep a pigeon away if it wants to reach its squabs in the nest," Haag-Wackernagel wrote; "motivation is simply too strong." Barriers can work if a building owner kills the squabs and clears out the nests. But even this only relocates the problem. The pigeon-control industry does steady work, pushing the birds along from one customer to the next. It's analogous (again) to the problem of homelessness: Cities try to solve the problem by hassling the homeless, telling them to move on. As a San Francisco cop once told me, "Every now and then a politician decides to sweep everyone out of one place and into another. And we're the broom." The pigeon-control businesses profit with every sweep.

There is another option for bird control: Cities have tried to exterminate pigeons with poison, traps, falcons, and even what Haag-Wackernagel calls a pigeon "electric chair"—essentially, a lethal electrified bird feeder. None of it has worked. For every pigeon that dies, another appears within days. The birds are simply too fecund: They reproduce so quickly that unless we were willing to kill the majority of birds in a city every year, we'd never make a dent.

The number of pigeons that live in a city, it turns out, is not determined by nesting space or by predation, but by the availability of food. After World War II, there was a revolution in agriculture: Munitions factories were retrofitted to produce fertilizer and food became cheap. Food became so abundant that people started throwing a lot of it away, often in places where pigeons could get at it.

Before World War II, pigeons filled their crops in daily flights from their nests in the cities to farms, or to seed-transport stations on the railways. This commute is a thing of the past. Pigeons now eat close to home, avoiding the long risky flight that made them vulnerable to predation by raptors.

No matter how plentiful the food, the population always grows until there are more beaks than crumbs. I watched that principle at work as pigeons fluttered down from perches around the park and gobbled up our bread.

"Papa," Josephine said plaintively, displaying her empty hands, "they need food."

The kind of feeding that Josephine was doing, tossing out the occasional crust or sharing a bit of lunch, is not significant enough to make a difference, according to Haag-Wackernagel.

The real problem is litter and massive regular feedings. When pigeons can come to a spot day in and day out for a guaranteed meal, their populations explode. And it's in this population explosion that the true problems arise. Roosting areas become crowded and filthy. Diseases and parasites spread. Birds become more aggressive. Shit splatters everywhere. Anyone who dares to toss out a little bread is immediately engulfed in a tornado of wings.

In 1988 Haag-Wackernagel helped the Swiss city of Basel launch the first truly successful pigeon-control program. The key component of this program was aimed not at pigeons, but at humans. It turned out that just a few individuals were responsible for the lion's share of feeding. These were mostly elderly, ragged folk for whom pigeon feeding is the central reason for being. They were covertly dumping pounds of grain, sometimes several times a day. "Pigeon feeders are often individuals who have no one to care for. The pigeons play an important role in replacing emotional ties," Haag-Wackernagel wrote in a report on the project. But it's not just unfortunate, slightly crazy people. Animal-rights groups and at least one neighborhood organization have reluctantly begun feeding large quantities of grain to pigeons because they feel a moral obligation to prevent the birds from starving. This is ridiculously wrongheaded, according to Haag-Wackernagel, because while feeding pigeons may indeed prevent some from starving, it increases the sum total of pigeon suffering. And so in Basel, Haag-Wackernagel helped authorities launch a campaign to teach the public that feeding pigeons is actually harmful to the species' population at large.

"We drastically demonstrated the negative effects of feeding, e.g., by pamphlets and posters showing shocking pictures of baby pigeons infected by diseases and parasites," Haag-Wackernagel wrote in another report. "We tried to explain the complicated relationship between feeding and overcrowding and the density-dependent causes of the poor living conditions."

All this made me reconsider my proposition that pigeons are innately revolting. It is humanity that has made pigeons disgusting. It is our own filth that has created the conditions that enable pigeon populations to swell to slum densities. In the end, there's only one way to control pigeons, Haag-Wackernagel, says: We have to control ourselves.

Forging Connections Deep in Pigeon Habitat

After we'd attracted our first flock of birds, I decided it was probably time to bring the feeding to an end. But this made no sense to Jo. I'd promised to let her feed the pigeons, I still had three-quarters of a slice of bread, and the birds were obviously still interested. They approached, bowing at every step, edging relentlessly forward. Pigeons have mastered a form of interspecies body language. There's something in the way that they approach that signals clearly to people that they are desperately interested in a snack. This language was crystal clear to my two-year-old: She was still learning the fundamentals of English, but she innately understood pigeon.

"They're super hungry," she repeated, imploringly.

We got the hang of feeding the pigeons eventually. The best technique was to let Jo dribble crumbs around my shoes so only the boldest of the birds would venture in, preventing a violent scrum.

The swarm dispersed, and the individuals that remained

wandered about with a relieving lack of intensity. We sat on a retaining wall, Josephine's feet dangling safely above a pair of black check pigeons, which scooted in to peck the bread, then scurried away again. The seagulls, less trusting, eyed us from a safe distance, a yard off.

When we ran out of bread, Jo wandered slowly into the park, following the birds. This time, though, instead of dashing manically, she settled onto her knees and watched. I sat and watched her watching.

A big, presumably male, pigeon had puffed out his neck feathers and was cooing assertively at a slimmer, presumably female, bird. The second bird kept inching away from his advances. I'd seen this scene acted out dozens of times, and I'd always assumed that I was witnessing courtship: a lothario pestering a girl who has no interest in him. But I'd learned that this is actually what's called driving. The birds were a mated pair, and the male was herding the female back to his own territory, where he wouldn't have to worry about other males competing for her affection. Courtship is more balanced. The males strut about, occasionally driving the females, bowing, and dragging their tails. But it's less bullying and insistent. In the end, it's the female who chooses among the males, and the pair solidifies their bond by feeding each other. The males' boorishness only becomes apparent after the birds are bonded for life. I wasn't going to try to convey any of this to Josephine quite yet.

I also did not tell her that, after mating, the male may, in Johnston's words, "stand tall, and then launch into a display flight," bringing his wings "smartly" together behind his back, clapping, presumably for himself. After reading this, I began to notice this clapping. Pigeons also clap their wings when straining to lift off vertically, but if it is a single bird making a triumphant ellipse of about a hundred feet and clapping periodically, I know.

An elderly Chinese man appeared from behind the sculpture, near where Jo knelt. He was feeding the pigeons too. I was too far away to understand the words that passed between him and Josephine, but each said something. They shared a moment of recognition, an acknowledgment of a mutual interest. These moments endear pigeons to the sociologist Colin Jerolmack, who appreciates the birds for their ability to bring very different people together. "I found that pigeon-feeding routines could become part of what Jane Jacobs called the 'intricate sidewalk ballet' that enriched pedestrians' experience," he wrote in his book *The Global Pigeon*. When people feed pigeons, he noticed, they also frequently strike up conversations with strangers who are doing the same. The opportunity to play with a wild thing provides some common ground for neighbors who may have nothing in common. This kind of casual shared experience is the foundation of friendship and, ultimately, of community. "While the child who takes heed of the birds around her might feel more connected to nature, she might also—or instead—feel more connected to her neighborhood," Jerolmack wrote.

I might have walked over to say hello myself, but at that moment I noticed two birds just a couple feet away on the retaining wall where I was sitting. Remembering my original mission, I peered at their feet, and indeed, one was missing a toenail (or talon, if you will), while the other had a sort of clubfoot. Both looked perfectly healthy otherwise. My imagination hadn't been embellishing pigeon deformities after all, or at least not generating them out of thin air. I snapped a few pictures. Then I lured Josephine into her stroller with the promise that we'd get ice cream in the ferry building before we went home.

A FEW FACTS TO SOFTEN HATRED OF PIGEONS

Feral pigeons are the same species as the birds bred to race, which have sold for more than $300,000 a bird. Those trained for racing can travel at up to 110 miles per hour for hours on end, propelled by massive breast muscles that constitute a third of their weight. Those breast muscles make them a culinary delicacy, and they are regularly served in fine restaurants. They have a mysterious ability to find their way home, no matter what scientists do to confuse them. Pigeons have received the highest military honors after delivering messages through storms of bullets. Pigeon post was the first major endeavor undertaken by one fledgling venture in journalism, which would become Reuters, the world's largest news-gathering organization. Pigeons mate for life, and can live to the age of twenty.

Heroes of Science and Battle

Perhaps the most remarkable thing about these birds is their ability to find their way home, even when the distances, the navigational challenges, and deadly obstacles are of epic proportions. Homing pigeons are the same species as street pigeons, they have simply been bred and trained for racing.

These thoroughbreds are about twice the weight of the average pigeon, and that mass resides mostly in the breast muscles.

Charlie Wolcott is perhaps the person who knows the most about pigeon navigation. He spent much of his scientific career confounded by the birds. He worked by coming up with hypotheses about the mechanism they use to find their way home, and then disabling that mechanism in test birds. If these handicapped birds didn't make it home, it would prove that he'd found their technique. For example, when Wolcott and his team thought that perhaps the birds were navigating by sight, using landmarks, they fitted them with frosted goggles. The pigeons came home—though many circled aimlessly in the last mile. (Apparently, sight is important in the homestretch.) When they guessed that the birds were using Earth's magnetic field to find their way, they strapped magnets to them. This had absolutely no effect. But when researchers strapped magnets to birds on a cloudy day, they were completely hornswoggled. This led Wolcott to a partial explanation:

"The pigeon uses [the] sun as a compass if it's a sunny day; if it's an overcast day, it switches and uses the earth's magnetic field as its compass."

Problem solved, right? Unfortunately, Wolcott said, finding the birds' compass was only half the solution. If you were dropped in the middle of the wilderness with a compass, which way would you go to get home? You would know which way was north, but you would have no idea if you were north of your home. So, in addition to a compass, you'd need a map. And with pigeons, the map remains utterly mysterious.

"There are at least three theories," Wolcott said. "One is

smell, and the Italians, appropriately, are great partisans of the olfactory hypothesis."

The idea is that the pigeons are mapping the sequence of smells as their handlers drive them out for a flight: "On the way to the release point you smell the odors as you go along, you pass olives, and then garlic, and then chocolate, the pines of Rome! You remember the sequence and they just go backwards," he said.

Then there's an idea that the birds are paying attention to the variations in magnetism, and they use these fluxes to build a map. So, odor and magnetism are the first two hypotheses: "The third is infrasound, very-low-frequency sound. Pigeons are sensitive to sounds down to one-tenth of one cycle per second. We [humans] quit at about twenty cycles per second. So pigeons are listening to these very low frequencies for reasons that we haven't a clue [about]."

But birds have made it home even after scientists disrupted their sense of smell, or messed with the magnetism, or interfered with their hearing. Scientists have anesthetized the birds, and put them on rotating turntables in airtight chambers, and driven them to the release site. "Oh yes, yes," Wolcott said. "We've done that. It doesn't bother them. The wretched creatures have several mechanisms, and when you take one away the little stinkers switch to something else," Wolcott said.

In his research Wolcott played the role of a James Bond villain, setting up impossible challenges, and inevitably the pigeons would dodge the alligators and flaming spikes without wrinkling their dinner jackets.

Pigeons have also, of course, played the role of unflappable government agents in real life. All those sensitive homing tools have allowed humans to put pigeons to use as instruments of communication, and they were particularly useful in war.

The most famous war pigeon is probably Cher Ami, who was trapped behind German lines with an American division during World War I. Back on the front lines, the US artillery, which had no clue the division was out there, was lobbing explosive shells onto American soldiers. The communications specialist for the trapped division released two pigeons. The Germans promptly shot them down. Then the Americans released Cher Ami, their last hope. Here's how Rose Wilder Lane embellished the drama of that moment in 1919 for the *Ladies' Home Journal*:

> Flung upward, . . . into stinging, blinding pain. For hardly had his wings taken hold of the air when agony struck him, stopped him, pierced him through and through. He fluttered and fell, fluttered, caught at the air and reeled. "God!" said the haggard man in the shell hole below. "He's done for."
>
> Convulsively the strong wings struck out again. Then they steadied and held the air. Cher Ami wavered, rose and wavered again. Then he vanished above the smoke. There was clear air around him. Beneath him was such a world as he had never seen, a hideous world without meaning or purpose. Only his wings were the wings he had known, and they carried him around and around, in weary circles.
>
> As he circled he heard a silent voice, a voice without words, that said: "Come!" "Come!" said the wordless message. "This is the right way. Follow it. Come!"

Every telling of this story I've read suffers from the same overindulgence in artistic license. It's just so potently heroic that writers can't help adding flourishes. Cher Ami made it back to the base in half an hour, but arrived missing an eye, and (aha!) a foot: The message canister on its leg was hanging by a few ligaments. But that was enough to save the soldiers. After Cher Ami died, a taxidermist preserved the body, and in doing so he found that Cher Ami was actually female—a transgender war hero. She's now at the Smithsonian. Cher Ami is pretty scruffy. On the street, she would be indistinguishable from any other one-legged pigeon. Now that we no longer have a use for these birds, they're considered bums. They're not so different from the grimy man carrying a piece of cardboard on which he's blocked out the words VETERAN, ANYTHING HELPS.

Carrier pigeons have gone out of fashion in the era of high-speed communication, but they may rise again. The Chinese military has trained ten thousand birds as a low-tech alternative in case their advanced communications technology is subverted or destroyed.

MYSTERY SOLVED

The mystery of mangled pigeon feet was maddeningly elusive. But finally, Haag-Wackernagle was able to supply a satisfying answer. I sent him the article that ran in *The Stranger,* which, he said, "contains a lot of nonsense but also the real reason: human hairs, fishing line, and other filaments get entangled, blood circulation stops, and necrosis leads to the loss of toes." Other birds don't have the same problem because they are better at removing hair with their beaks, whereas pigeons seem unable to rid themselves of the filaments. In addition, other birds hop while pigeons walk. Pigeons shuffle along in a way that makes them more likely to pick up strings than a skipping sparrow. The explanation is, in the end, quite simple, he said. Still, there is no end to speculation: "In Germany people believed that a mysterious person would hogtie pigeons," he said.

Everyone who studies pigeons long enough seems to gain some affection for them, and I was no different. To Johnston and Janiga they are a "masterpiece." Haag-Wackernagle wrote a richly illustrated coffee-table book documenting their natural history and the roles they have played in art and religion. At the end of my conversation with Wolcott, I asked him if there was anything else I should be thinking about, and he delivered a lovely little soliloquy on the strange alien world he has been able to glimpse by watching pigeons:

"One of the things we all naively assume about animals is that they live in the same world that we do, and they see things the way we do. And it's very clear pigeons are not like that. For example, they are exquisitely sensitive to changes in [atmospheric] pressure. They can tell the difference between the floor and the ceiling in the room I'm sitting in—maybe eight feet of vertical displacement. We can feel it in our ears when we go in an elevator up these big skyscrapers, but we're amateurs compared to your average street pigeon. They can hear down to these very low frequencies. Pigeons have the ability to see in the ultraviolet, which we do not. Pigeons have the ability to sense, somehow, Earth's magnetic field. Pigeons can detect the plane of polarized light, something we have real trouble doing. Those are just some of the things that come to mind. So they live in a very different world, in a way. It's fun to think about what that world an animal inhabits is like, and what kind of information it's getting there, and why it matters."

Want to open the doors of perception? You could experiment with psychedelics, or you could look to that underappreciated portal to extrasensory awareness: the pigeon. When I first started thinking about pigeons I saw only filth and pestilence. But what I was really seeing was human failings—poverty, waste, and our refusal to stop feeding these birds while shirking all the other responsibilities that come with domestication. But thanks to Wolcott I can now see them as antennae picking up signals beyond our ken. They are war heroes to me now, champion racers and devoted parents. It was disgust that drove me to pigeons, but I feel true affection for them now.

WEEDS

AS SHE NEARED HER THIRD birthday, Josephine made a ritual of riding her plastic tricycle before dinner. She'd roll toward the BART station, gathering smiles from commuters walking home. Every day she would pedal about two blocks before deciding she would prefer to find something filthy on the sidewalk to put in her mouth. And then I would carry both her and the tricycle home.

One day, as she was transitioning out of the riding phase, and scanning the ground for something suitably vile to eat, I noticed an exuberant stand of wild fennel growing beside a telephone pole. Wild fennel springs up wherever there is exposed dirt in my neighborhood. It doesn't form bulbs like the fennel you see in supermarkets, but its feathery leaves are sweet, and taste like licorice.

Sensing an opportunity to channel Josephine's attraction away from sidewalk detritus, I plucked a tender shoot and held it out to her. "Do you know what this plant is?"

She shook her head gravely.

"Fennel. Some people call it candy plant."

"Candy plant?"

I had her attention. I handed her the sprig.

"Can I eat it?" she asked.

And for once, I could say yes. Of course, it's not totally safe to eat wild plants growing on the street: They could be contaminated with heavy metals, or covered with exhaust, or spritzed with dog pee. But with most things, the dose makes the poison and a little bit wouldn't hurt her, especially relative to what she gets into on a daily basis. Dog pee isn't actually hazardous to people, and I'd picked my sprig from near the top of the plant, some four feet off the ground.

Josephine gingerly nibbled the fennel. Then she put the whole thing between her lips and chewed. Then, before I could protest, she pulled two big handfuls of older, tougher greens from lower down—tall-dog height—and wadded them into her mouth.

I have a fantasy about being the kind of father who notices on his commute that the chestnuts on a nearby tree are ripe and brings home an armful to roast—the kind of person who is able to gather up richness where others see nothing worth noting. And so I began studying the edible plants around me. You need local guidebooks to identify plants because there are so many that look alike. But many of the things that are good to eat travel with humans, springing up in the landscapes we disturb. Many of the edible weeds related to dandelions, for instance—bristly oxtongue, prickly lettuce, chicory, hairy cat's ear—have spread around the world with people.

It turned out that the oxalis, or wood sorrel, which seemed to spring from the earth as fast as I could pull it out, had a pleasantly tart taste. Josephine would command me to stop the stroller and bound off into the underbrush to harvest this "sour grass" and "candy plant." We agreed that she would pick only the new growth—fresh young plants were less likely to have something nasty on them, I figured—and I taught her to make her selections from places that would not attract dogs. A few germs and impurities, I decided, were a worthwhile trade-off for the fun of eating out of the parks and unkempt front yards in our neighborhood.

DELICIOUS DANDELIONS?

I came to this study of edible plants with some skepticism about urban foraging. It seems to me that the sort of people who are excited about eating wild plants are also the sort given to the credulous acceptance of myths. There are three types of foragers in particular that bug me: the survivalists, the herbalists, and the taste-bud-less.

The survivalists are the ones with the misconception that they could someday subsist on plantain heads and dock leaves. If they were actually put to the test, most of these people would end up starving like Rebecca Lerner. She describes her experiment in eating only what she could gather in her book, *Dandelion Hunter*. After a week of living off the land in Portland, she wrote: "My body was achy and limp. My legs were so weak that I had to brace myself against the wall like an old lady who lost her walker."

Lerner eventually gave in and feasted on Thai food, noting, "There's a thin line between badass and dumbass."

The herbalists are the ones who insist on telling me that such and such is good for the liver, or will flush out my toxins. I'm a fan of alternative medicine, but when I'm trying to learn something I like my information to be evidence based. But when someone tells me earnestly that echinacea cures colds (even though I know it's been studied to death and ultimately looks like a good placebo), it makes me doubt everything else I'm learning from them.

Then there's the taste-bud-less: The folks that munch on tough old dandelions and proclaim them delicious. As Tama Matsuoka Wong writes in her book, *Foraged Flavor*, "It was pretty easy to find nature-oriented books that told me which of these plants are 'edible,' but my quest instead was for plants that actually taste *good*" (her italics). One of the books in the vein is *Edible Wild Plants of Eastern North America*, coauthored by Alfred C. Kinsey; it contains a comprehensive listing of species, but doesn't tell you what to do with them. The same might be said, incidentally, of Kinsey's more famous reports on human sexuality, which include plenty of facts, but no advice for the lay reader on putting them into practice.

There are lots of plants that the experts advise you to boil three times in three different batches of water, i.e., things you'd only eat if you were starving. The highest praise in many guides is mildness, the ability of a plant to pass through your mouth undetected. The foraging literature frequently ignores flavor, and there's a touch of apocalyptic asceticism in many of the guidebooks I've leafed through. They carry the implication that, come the revolution, there will be no place for those who hesitate to scarf down hairy bittercress.

But we shouldn't let the three breeds of hyperbolic foragers out there spoil what, done right, can be a truly good thing. The existence of survivalists, herbalists, and the taste-bud-less did nothing to stint the pleasure I got from foraging as a kid: In the Sierra foothills my friends and I would eat blackberries, pine nuts, and manzanita flowers in the spring and their powdery, sunbaked berries in the fall. We never expected to fill our bellies on this stuff, but it felt good to know it was there, to be able to find the landscape's sweetness, and to think of the previous civilizations that had foraged there.

Experienced foragers understand that you can't actually survive on wild salads alone: It's fruits, nuts, seeds, roots, and meat that provide the calories. Lerner eventually finds her foraging groove, and with the help of a small village of friends, assembles a Thanksgiving feast. She writes, "It was an impressive display: rose hips sauce, roasted cattail, nettle, mushrooms, wapato, venison, scones, and even wild beer."

I'd be pleased to get that at a fancy San Francisco restaurant. And of course, the finest restaurants are serving foraged weeds already. Daniel, the New York eatery with two Michelin stars, and Copenhagen's Noma, often called the best restaurant in the world, both rely on foraged foods, tapping the flavors and textures of things people normally don't think of as food.

The success of those restaurants renewed my interest in foraging. I don't want to be the sort of guy who tries to make his family eat "actually, starvation sounds pretty good right now" salads. But Wong, who forages for Daniel, has published a book full of recipes for and advice on turning weeds into high cuisine, which kindled my hope that I might make meals a little more delicious with a touch of the wild.

We've reached a strange point in history when foraging, once a stopgap for the desperately poor, is now firmly associated with upper-class food—so much so that it's impossible to say you are serving, for example, foraged sheep sorrel or wild fennel sprigs without sounding a bit pretentious. This is bizarre: I can't afford to eat at either Daniel or Noma, but wild plants are free.

EAT YOUR YARD

There's an effort at the University of California, Berkeley, to connect the people with the least money to the highfalutin ingredients growing in the cracks in their driveways. Philip Stark, a Berkeley statistics professor, organized a team of researchers to map edible plants in low-income neighborhoods with the goal of creating a Web site that will show residents how to find food close to their homes.

In the United States, poverty is highly correlated with obesity and diet-related disease. If poor people actually found it feasible to eat foraged greens, the public health benefit could be immense. And incidentally, the places labeled food deserts—low-income neighborhoods without markets—are also the places where Stark is finding the most edible weeds. "The hypothesis is that the food is already there," he said. "It's just not recognized as food."

I asked Stark if I could tag along with him sometime when he went out looking at plants, which he said he does nearly every day. We met at his home in the Berkeley hills and strolled the winding roads.

A walk with a forager is not leisurely. Stark did not gaze at the vistas or remark on the architectural details of the houses we passed. Instead, he stared intently at the margins of the road, and regularly broke off in midsentence to dash to one side or the other to inspect something green and nondescript. He is tall, lean, and balding, with close-shorn hair about the length of the stubble on his cheeks. He wore sandals—a simple sole attached to his foot with leather laces—loose gray pants, and a rust-orange Arc'teryx windbreaker. He rattled off Latin and common names faster than I could write them down. "*Lactuca virosa*," he said, squatting and plucking a hairy leaf. "Opium lettuce, or bitter lettuce." He put it in his mouth and chewed. I did the same. It was bitter, not overwhelmingly so, but also not something I'd want to eat in bulk. "I actually quite like things with stronger flavors," Stark said. He'll use a bitter leaf or two like a spice, to punctuate an otherwise conventional omelet or piece of meat.

A little farther on we came to a sloping triangle of dirt between a driveway and the road. Stark began listing the edible species there. "Bristly oxtongue, curly dock, miner's lettuce, mallow, fennel, chickweed, sow thistle, cow parsnip, wood sorrel, nasturtium—here's a ten-ingredient salad, more than you could get in a mixed-mesclun bag at the farmers' market. And it's free."

On the second day of official fieldwork for the project, Stark told me, he and his compatriots bumped into another team looking for precisely the same plants. It was a team of city workers in haz-mat suits spraying herbicide to kill the greens. They were in West Oakland, home to a lot of people whose diets would surely be improved by eating those weeds. Here were two problems—people in need of free healthy foods and weeds in need of removal—that might be resolved with a single solution.

There are still issues to sort out. First, is it safe to eat greens growing amid paint chips, auto exhaust, dog piss, and the mysterious fallout of urban grime? Second, will the people who most need more greens in their diet have the time to forage for, wash, and cook them?

Stark is running a battery of tests to answer the first question. Plants do absorb pollutants, but it's unclear if they take in enough to cause concern. The second question is tougher. Foraging makes perfect sense if you are cash poor and time rich. But it makes no sense when you're working three jobs and still broke. Several attempts to fix food deserts have failed because the problem isn't simply that people lack access to vegetables; they also may not have the skills to make them delicious, or the time to prepare them.

THE FATHER OF WEED EATERS

Still, there's often at least one person in a household who might have time to forage, even if it's a child. In 1922, Euell Theophilus Gibbons was a child, and his family was starving. His father had left their homestead in rural New Mexico to look for work, and his mother was sick because, rather than eating, she was giving the food she had to her four children. The horse died, and the family dog ate her. Then the eleven-year-old Gibbons went out looking for food—and found it. He found rabbits and prickly pears, mushrooms and berries. He fed his family every day for a month until his father returned. And then he kept on foraging.

Forty years later, after hoboing, and picking cotton, and busting broncos, and working as a Communist agitator, Euell

Gibbons wrote a book about foraging titled *Stalking the Wild Asparagus*. It was a bestseller. It's this book that planted the romance of foraging into our culture, setting the taproot for the later flowering of foraged dishes at restaurants like Daniel. The seed of our current fascination with foraging was a hungry kid searching the New Mexico desert for something he could bring home for his mother.

DELICIOUS INVADERS

Gibbons counseled that the deep wilderness is a poor place to go looking for food. The best spots, he wrote, are "old fields, fence rows, burned-off areas, roadsides, along streams, woodlots, around farm ponds, swampy areas and even vacant lots." Many of the plants that are good for people to eat have traveled with us. Dandelion seeds came to the New World on the *Mayflower*, though historians don't know if they were for use as medicine or food. (Dandelions can provide real sustenance if you dig up their starchy roots, rather than trying to eat their leaves.)

I tend to dislike invasive plants, because they take over and crowd out diversity. But when I began to look closely at these weeds, I saw a lot to admire. They can grow in incredibly hostile environments, without water, fertilizer, or even soil. They grow despite the fact that people frequently pull them up and poison them. They are tough, versatile, and resilient. And, as Wong points out, the chemicals that make these weeds strong also give them the powerful flavors prized by chefs. There's something about these flavorful plants that seems to improve the health of the people who eat them. These phytochemicals are mysterious because many of them are poisons produced by plants to defend against being eaten. But the theory is that because humans evolved eating low doses of these toxins, we need them: They trigger a stress response, much like exercise does, and give your system a workout.

Eating weeds has allowed me to engage with the natural world in a new way. I chew on peppery nasturtium leaves on my way to work. When I'm making a sandwich and realize we're out of greens, I just go outside and pick some. I pluck unfamiliar plants and take them home for identification.

When Josephine learned which species she could eat, this knowledge worked transformative magic upon her: At mealtime, she normally rejects anything green, but she'll happily sample what she gathers. As a passive recipient of food, there's no incentive for her to eat anything but the most pleasing flavors. But when she seeks out her own food, it produces a pronounced shift in cognition. If I serve her something unfamiliar, she acts as if I'm trying to poison her. When she's sampling wild leaves, on the other hand, she grows intensely contemplative, pondering the challenging new flavors. I suspect it's true for us all, not just toddlers: It's as much human nature to resist novelty when someone else is trying to force it on us, as it is to open ourselves to novelty when we are seeking it for ourselves.

"Once your brain registers that there's food out there, your brain starts interacting with the environment in a different way," Stark told me. What was once just a green jumble in every unmown verge began to come into focus as soon as I had a good reason to pay attention to these weeds. Josephine, who never learned *not* to see these plants, can identify almost as many species as I can. As a game, I'll sit on our stoop and send her off to search for sorrel or dock, and a few minutes later she'll come running back with the correct leaf. It still seems miraculous to me that toddlers—all of us, actually—can find one nondescript plant among many. When you learn about an edible plant, something clicks into place. Here's how Gibbons described it to the writer John McPhee: "It is exactly like recognizing someone's face; once you know a person, you know that person from all other people. If you came home at night and a woman you had never seen was standing there in your house, you wouldn't think it was your wife. God help you, anyway, if you would."

The contemplative pleasures of getting to know my natural neighbors is a middle-class luxury. I don't think I'd be taking the time to learn and taste my weeds if I was a single parent hustling to get my kids fed and into bed. I might, however, have the time if I were a child of that single parent—like Gibbons. There's often at least one person in a household who could make time to forage if they knew how, or had a good mentor.

There's a sense of satisfaction that comes with finding food to help support your family. I'm not talking like a survivalist here; there's no way people in West Oakland are going to get the bulk of their calories from weeds anytime soon. I'm just pointing out that a small helping of foraged greens each day could make people healthier, even if it's layered on a fast-food hamburger to provide some crunch.

There are many evangelical books, usually based on little science, extolling the healing benefits of wild plants. There's no need to make airy claims about the superpowers of plants when we can instead point to the well-established benefits of eating leafy green vegetables. We'd all be healthier, poor and middle class alike, if we could open our eyes to the natural world around us and see the richness there that we usually miss. If by foraging we simply hope to harvest a little pleasure and a connection to the wild, the chances of success are good. But the likelihood of success declines if we're primarily gathering food for the body rather than the soul.

Can we harvest our way to health, equality, and justice from the wild things around us? Not with weeds alone. That would require concerted political action. But we'd be well served by foraging among the weeds for symbols to fuel that action. The garden the Obamas dug into the White House lawn became a symbol of the struggle to get fresh, healthy foods into the hands of ordinary Americans. I'm a supporter of gardens in general, and of that garden specifically. But I'd like to point out that it was preceded by other symbols on the White House lawn. Once, many years before anyone knew the name Obama, Euell Gibbons put his arm through the fence surrounding the White House to pick four different edible plants. The food is there, and so are the symbols, if we have eyes to see them.

SQUIRREL

JOSEPHINE AND I WERE VENTURING furtively down the pea-gravel driveway of some unknown neighbor to examine the ground beneath the outermost circumference of a great oak. I had told Josephine we were collecting acorns, but I had an ulterior motive: I hoped to find the half-eaten acorns that served as clues to a mystery I'd discovered in my squirrel books. Josephine was in it simply for the joy of acorns. She delights in the geometric curiosities produced by trees and bushes (seedpods, catkins, drupes) and occasionally will bring them home for me. I keep these gifts on my desk until they burst open or otherwise turn into a mess.

When I'd asked Josephine if she had any interest in joining me in an acorn hunt, she replied, "Of course!"

She had just turned three and was all blond curls and dimples. She was wearing a purple dress with a horse on the front that she'd gotten for her birthday. It was just long enough to hide the dirt on her knees, but not long enough to cover the scabs from the mosquito bites she'd scratched till they'd bled.

The oaks in our neighborhood are coast live oaks, an evergreen species that produces sharp, bulletlike acorns. When

young, these acorns are green at the pointed end fading to but-
tery yellow under the cap. They are silky smooth to the touch.

There were no acorns under the first few trees. Then we
came to a big oak hanging over a driveway, and there they
were everywhere. I ventured a few steps onto the gravel to
retrieve one, and then a few more for another. Josephine scam-
pered ahead of me, between two parked cars. I looked at the
acorns in my hand. Just as I'd hoped, each had a bite taken out
of it, near the top.

I was looking for something that Michael Steele, a squirrel
researcher at Wilkes University, had noticed back in 1986. He
was checking on squirrel nest boxes in a forest in the Sandhills
of North Carolina when he and his companions noticed something strange. That year, the turkey oaks had produced a "dense
blanket of acorns in the leaf litter." Nut trees and conifers periodically produce these bumper crops in what's called a mast
year. When the researchers knelt to investigate they saw that
"each of the thousands of acorns was partially eaten, not in a
haphazard way but neatly and consistently from the top," Steele
later wrote. That night, after they'd finished counting squirrels
in nest boxes, they sat around and puzzled over the acorns. The
mystery was, as Steele wrote, "why would any squirrel, or any
animal for that matter, invest the energy to eat a small portion
of a single food item, only to pick up another and repeat the
process?" The squirrel chips away the tough outer shell to
expose the acorn meat, then only takes half the payment promised for its labor. Why?

When they returned to Wake Forest University (where Steele
was teaching at the time) they found the same thing: half-eaten

acorns beneath the local willow oaks. Steele grabbed a handful of acorns and took them to a university museum, where he found some squirrel skulls. The incisors fit the tooth marks in the acorns perfectly.

When Josephine returned, she carried two more acorns, each marked by what looked like an incisor bite that pierced the shell of the acorn, but then went no farther. It was just a single bite, which was different from what Steele had seen: The acorns he had found were precisely half-eaten. When I asked Steele about the single-bite acorns Josephine and I had found, he said we were looking at something different. "Right now, the acorns are still developing and the squirrels are sampling the tissue," he said. In other words, squirrels, tempted by not-quite-ripe acorns, opened the shell, took a bite, and (blech!) threw it to the ground.

Steele has blue eyes, a graying goatee, and a gentle manner. He became a squirrel expert almost by accident; his real interest is relationships—the diplomacy and deals negotiated between plants and animals that end up shaping entire landscapes. When Steele began asking around about acorns, he told me, researchers from around the county said they were seeing squirrels— and birds too—leaving acorns half-uneaten, especially during mast years.

On a hunch, the researchers tried sprouting the half-eaten seeds. Lo and behold, they germinated, and for some species, more sprouted from the half-eaten seeds than from the ones left whole. Every species relies on partnerships to survive. It seems that oak trees and squirrels had worked out a deal: The squirrels get to eat acorns, but not the whole nut. In return, the squirrels disperse the seeds, and even bury some of them. Perhaps squirrels are planning generations ahead, planting the next crop of oaks.

SQUIRRELS AND TREES

The reason for a squirrel is redistribution. It is a great leveler of abundance and scarcity: a shock absorber in rodent from. The squirrel's body and character were shaped by the overriding factor in their existence: their evolutionary partnership with trees, which produce a lot of their food all at once, and then nothing for the rest of the year. And so everything about a squirrel is focused on the imperative to turn boom and bust into steady living.

Squirrels eat a lot of other things besides tree nuts: plants, underground fungi, insects, bones, sometimes baby birds, and even in some cases each other. Some catch fish. But they have a special relationship with nut trees. When there are plenty of nuts, squirrel populations swell, and when nuts are scarce, they die. Like humans, they make supplies last by harvesting and storing. A lot of animals simply sleep through the lean times by building up fat when food is abundant and then hibernating, but not tree squirrels. The species that live in our cities stay active all winter. They eat as much as they can in the fall and put on a layer of fat, but it only amounts to about 10 percent of their body weight. That's the equivalent of a 180-pound guy like me gaining 18 pounds—a lot, but not enough to last all winter.

Squirrels are much better at burning fat than gaining it. When temperatures drop, some internal switch flips and they begin to turn fat into heat thirteen and a half times faster than normal. This performance "stands as one of the best among animals," according to Steele and his fellow squirrel researcher John Koprowski of the University of Arizona. Without even moving, they then can produce energy like a pro cyclist powering up into the Pyrenees.

And so squirrels are able to smooth out the fluctuation between scarcity and abundance, first by hiding away calories in food caches, and then by converting this fuel in an efficient internal furnace.

Hibernation might seem like a safer strategy, but hibernation is inflexible. If someone destroys your home in the middle of a three-month nap, you are dead. As climate change shifts the timing of winter temperatures, many hibernating species are struggling. Belding's ground squirrels in Yosemite, for example, rely on a thick layer of snow to insulate their burrows during hibernation, and they have been killed when an unseasonable thaw floods their nests. By staying awake, city squirrels are better able to adapt to changing conditions and take advantage of disrupted patterns. Small wonder that they thrive alongside humans, since our survival strategy is the same.

From another perspective, however, it is a great wonder that squirrels thrive alongside us because they were shaped before the first *Homo sapiens* ever walked the earth. They are identical to the squirrels that lived five million years ago, as far as biologists can tell. This, then, is the second great squirrel mystery: How is it that these ancient beasts have managed to thrive in our cities when so many other species have simply died off?

Memory

One cloudy morning I arrived at a coffee shop across the street from the UC Berkeley campus to meet Mikel Delgado. Delgado is a grad student who studies squirrels, which means that, rather than traveling to the rain forest to trap butterflies or scuba diving to observe whales, her subject of research is directly outside her door. Squirrel habitat is almost 100 percent coincident with student habitat.

She was waiting for me at an outside table, wearing a brown Carhartt sweatshirt, a green knit scarf, and purple glasses with gray checked temples. Her hair was black, with a few strands of white, and pulled back. She smiled and suggested we walk to her office.

"I've only just begun my research," I told her. "You can assume total ignorance."

She scanned for squirrels as we strolled, and seemed disappointed when they did not immediately appear. "It's still early," she said. "They may not be up yet. They are adapted to the schedules of the students."

That is, because the people around them are not early risers, neither are the squirrels. They are attuned to their food sources' rhythms, whether they be the seasonal production of tree nuts or the time of day at which college students are most likely to flip pizza crusts toward a charming tree kitten.

A pair of crows called from a treetop as we approached, and Delgado explained that squirrels react to crow alarm calls. The crows seem to sense danger a little sooner than squirrels do.

When we got to her lab, Delgado opened a big plastic tub filled with neatly partitioned nuts. She stowed a few handfuls of these in a fanny pack: pecans, walnuts, and almonds, all in their shells.

As soon as we emerged we began seeing squirrels. "Watch this," she said, tossing a nut to one that approached us. "You'll see he turns it 'round and 'round in his mouth, and he's just feeling for what's the best way to carry it, and maybe also checking for imperfections in the shell. If it's cracked he might eat it right now rather than burying it and having it go bad."

"How do they crack something like a walnut?" I asked.

"They have incredibly strong jaws. Before I started studying squirrels I got bitten by one while feeding it, and it really hurt. They have poor close vision, so they can't see which is the nut and which is the finger. They have relatively clean mouths, they don't often carry rabies, but they can carry other diseases, so it's not a good idea to touch them."

As she was saying this, another squirrel approached and pawed at my pant leg. "Step back!" I cried.

Delgado tossed a walnut directly at the beast's head. It dodged nimbly and picked up its reward.

"So he'll turn it," Delgado said, "and then if you watch carefully, they do this headshake."

I watched.

"There."

I had seen nothing.

"It's very fast. There was a student here, Stephanie Preston"—now a professor of psychology at the University of Michigan—"who first noticed it. All these squirrel scientists had been observing them for years and no one had ever described this."

It took me a good half hour of close watching before I saw it.

A few months later, watching videos of squirrels, I found it had become invisible to me again, and it only reappeared after I watched a video in slow motion.

It's almost a flinch, a jerk over one shoulder and back. Scientists still aren't sure why they do this; maybe they get a sense for the quality of the nut by rattling it in its shell. If insects have partially eaten an acorn, a squirrel will eat it immediately (along with the insects) rather than burying it.

Delgado studies the way squirrels store food. Different species have different food-storage strategies. First, there are the larder hoarders, which put all their nuts in one place and defend it. Then there are the scatter hoarders, and city squirrels fall in this category. It's a diversified investment strategy: If someone else pillages a storage place, they lose just one nut. The problem with scatter hoarding is that squirrels end up with thousands of nuts all over the place, and they have to remember precisely where each one is, or else it's gone forever.

It's impossible to compass the enormity of this problem unless you've tried to do what a squirrel does. Forget about remembering the locations of thousands of nuts—do you suppose you could remember a single location? And to make things easier, instead of remembering that location for three or four years, as squirrels do, do you think you could remember it for just, say, five seconds? When I tried to do it, it resulted in utter, humiliating failure.

The squirrel had taken Delgado's nut about fifteen feet away. It scratched at the surface for a couple seconds, deposited the nut, and then bent over to tamp it down with its teeth, arching its back and pumping twice. Then it brushed some dirt and pine needles over the spot and was off. The whole operation was over in a quarter minute.

Delgado suggested we try to find the nut. At first, this seemed a little bit unsporting. After all, I'd never taken my eyes off the spot where the squirrel had been. But I gamely walked over. Then, as I crouched down, something curious happened. The ground in front of me dissolved into an undifferentiated pattern of sticks and leaves and tufts of grass. Had the squirrel been right here? Or was it perhaps a half foot to my right? That actually looked more likely, and that's where there was a bit of pine needle duff overturned, with the wet underside facing the sun. I brushed this away, but there was no sign of disturbed soil. I dug up a bit of ground with a stick. Nothing. Compacted clay. The idea that a squirrel had just made a hole there seemed impossible. I turned back toward my original spot, but I couldn't pinpoint it now, and I noticed glumly that Delgado was searching several feet away. I disconsolately turned over more leaf litter. It was utterly hopeless. I'd have to dig up yards of dirt to find this nut. It did make me feel a little better when Delgado came up empty as well. Often she does find the buried nut, but not always. "This is just something that squirrels have evolved to be very good at," she said. "Hiding nuts is one of their specialties."

For many years researchers suspected that squirrels actually did not remember where they buried their nuts, and instead simply sniffed the ground until they located any subterranean stash at random. But the leader of Delgado's lab, Lucia Jacobs, showed that this was not the case. Squirrels do sometimes stumble across (and eat) the nuts of others, but the vast majority of the time they dig up the nuts that they themselves have stored.

Henry Thoreau wondered at this as he tromped through the snow around Concord, Massachusetts. "In almost every wood, you will see where the red or gray squirrels have pawed down through the snow in a hundred places, sometimes two feet deep, and almost always directly to a nut or pine-cone, as directly as if they had started from it and bored upward."

The problem here is not just that you have to remember that there's a nut buried under the juniper bush (as it was in this case), you have to remember precisely which square inch under the juniper bush it is. Then multiply that by five thousand. Delgado wonders if it's based on some kind of geometric mnemonic, with each squirrel filling in dots that sketch a shape, perhaps a giant spiral.

Squirrels versus Trees

This brings us back to the mystery of the half-eaten acorns. The mystery must touch, in some way, the symbiotic relationship between squirrel and oak.

No matter how good the memories of squirrels, they fail to retrieve some seeds in periods when their larders outlast the hungry times. And when a squirrel dies, its trove might eventually grow into a forest. Squirrels provide a service to trees by distributing and burying their seeds far beyond the patch of dirt where they fell. Acorns buried by squirrels have a much better chance of growing into sprouts than those that fall atop the leaf litter.

But these mutually beneficial deals are never completely harmonious. In nature, no species ever settles on the terms of a

partnership for long. Instead, the parties are constantly renego-
tiating their agreements, always edging for a slightly better deal.
The oak and the squirrel aren't exactly allies. I started thinking
of them as a pair of crusty old Hollywood producers: They've
known each other since they were young, have profited tremendously from doing business together, and they enjoy joshing each
other with affectionate obscenities over drinks. But each loves
nothing more than finding some devious way to cheat the other.

White oaks, for example, made what looks like a bid to
game the terms of the coevolutionary contract by producing
acorns that germinate rapidly, sprouting soon after they are buried. To thwart this strategy and still reap the energy in the nut-
meat, squirrels eat these nondormant seeds rather than burying
them. When they do decide to bury a nondormant acorn, they
first gnaw out the embryo, transforming the seed into an inert
mass of calories that cannot sprout.

Steele and other scientists investigating half-eaten acorns
have found that an acorn has more fats, which squirrels like, in
its top half, and in its bottom half, around the embryo, there are
more tannins, which squirrels dislike. Tannins—the same chemicals that make wines "dry"—are poisonous in high concentra-
tions. They are a mainstay of plant chemical warfare, used by
everything from apples to persimmons. That feeling of all the
moisture being sucked out of your mouth when you bite into an
acorn or an unripe apple comes from the tannins you've just
released, which act as molecular vacuum cleaners, hoovering up
all the proteins that make your saliva feel slippery. Unlike squirrels, humans can't eat acorns without processing the tannins.

The researchers thought they'd found the answer: The oak

trees are giving the squirrels half of each acorn, yet protecting the important bits. And, it seemed, guiding the squirrels to the more delicious half of the acorn with its shape. When a researcher whittled acorns so the top looked like the bottom and vice versa, the squirrels ate the wrong end: the one containing more tannins, less fats, and most importantly, the embryo. Squirrels use the shape of an acorn to find the tastier end, just as we use the shape of an apple to bite into the flesh rather than the core. If a team of devious scientists reshaped our apples so the core ran widthwise, we might find ourselves inadvertently eating it.

When squirrels are hungry, they always eat the whole acorn. But when there is an abundance of them, they will just eat the best part and discard the rest. This may explain the evolutionary logic behind a mast year: By producing gigantic pulses of nuts, oak trees ensure that some of their acorns will make it past the predators. The same logic drives trees, even in normal years, to produce all their nuts or fruits within a small window of time. The tree evolved toward boom and bust. The squirrel is a shock absorber. By working to bamboozle each other, they work together.

SQUIRRELS AND PEOPLE

Of course, squirrels eat more than acorns, and their options are especially diverse when they live among humans. Humans frequently put out buffets of seeds from which squirrels can eat their fill. The humans, however, usually intend these seeds for wild birds and view the squirrels as unwanted guests. You probably know some of these humans.

There's a whole genre of Internet videos and forums dedicated to the contest between humans and squirrels for control over bird feeders. I have a book on the subject: *Outwitting Squirrels: 101 Cunning Stratagems to Reduce Dramatically the Egregious Misappropriation of Seed from Your Birdfeeder by Squirrels*, by Bill Adler Jr. The fact that humans must summon this much collective brainpower and earnest scheming to match wits with a one-pound rodent says something not so complimentary about us. At the end of his book, Adler urges his readers not to give up and admit defeat:

> I have high hopes for civilization. We have survived world wars, the cold war, devastating plagues. We have gone to the moon, and sent probes past the outermost edge of our solar system. We have eliminated major diseases, and we have invented *Wheel of Fortune*.
>
> But only if we keep up our struggle to outwit squirrels can humankind expect to progress towards the next level of development, whatever that may be.

Late one night, lost deep in the Internet of squirrels, I stumbled across a series of videos by Steve Barley that offered an admirable alternative to the no-holds-barred warfare I'd grown used to seeing, and I was moved to write to him.

Barley, who lives in suburban Hertfordshire, England, entered into his relationship with squirrels in the traditional way: They destroyed his bird feeders, and he got annoyed and started looking for ways to stop them.

His local squirrels severed the rope supporting one feeder, sending it crashing to the ground. Squirrel incisors also made

quick work of his plastic feeders. Next, Barley bought steel feeders covered in wire mesh. Of course these didn't deter them
either. But as Barley watched the squirrels dismantling the
defenses, instead of growing angry, he began to feel something
resembling admiration.

"It was only when I watched them figure out how to hang
upside down on the wire mesh "squirrel-proof" ones and then
widen a hole low down with their teeth and claws to get the nuts
out like in a gumball machine that I began to respect their inge-
nuity and acrobatic skills," he told me.

"They were fascinating to watch, especially the way they can
reverse their rear claws to hang on with ease, leaving their front
paws to do their stuff."

Squirrels have hinged ankles that rotate 180 degrees. For
comparison, imagine a ballet dancer going up on pointe; that's
not quite ninety degrees. This flexibility allows squirrels to
drape themselves over the shields and baffles employed by some
bird feeders. Squirrels also have the right sort of brain for this
sort of thing. They are problem solvers, Delgado had told me,
motivated and persistent. And though they lack opposable
thumbs, they have good motor skills and dexterous fingers.

As Barley and his son were watching the squirrels empty the
feeders, he hit upon the idea of hanging one off a clothesline,
just to see how they would manage it. This was not much of a
challenge: The squirrels made what had looked like an impossible leap from a bird platform. At this point, Barley's annoy-
ance ceded to curiosity: How much could these squirrels do?

"We experimented with a piece of trellis," Barley said, "and they jumped onto that to reach the feeder hanging further down the line." He and his son were playing *with* the squirrels now rather than against them, and kept adding bits and pieces to the collection of obstacles: an old ironing board, a plunger, a bicycle mudguard, a lampshade, and on and on.

They filmed squirrels making short work of this obstacle course, and, as is the way with these things, it ended up on You-Tube, where it became a minor sensation.

As amusing as Barley's contraptions are, they don't truly test the outer limits of what squirrels are capable of doing. The closest we have ever come to accomplishing that was in 1999, when the BBC built an obstacle course for a series about squirrels called *Daylight Robbery* (Barley hadn't seen it when he started building his own in 2010).

To beat this course, squirrels had to climb up through a vertical pipe, leap onto a blade of a spinning windmill, cling to it, and then sail off on the right trajectory to land on a platform. Then they had to go paw over paw upside down along a suspended chain that passed through a series of spinning disks, negotiate a revolving door, run through a slack canvas tube, and keep their balance while crossing a pole covered with slick spinning rollers. From there, it was a six-foot jump to another tunnel, through which they had to ride a sliding vehicle made to look like a rocket ship by pushing it along with their paws. Finally, there was an eight-foot jump to the food.

This challenge took the squirrels a little over a month to figure out. They mastered the obstacles with varying levels of grace—one female learned to complete the course without hesitation or error each time she tried, earning her the starring role in the production.

Despite their skills, squirrels are not known for their cunning, or their athleticism. Squirrels are known for their teeth: They have no canines, so they have their distinctive incisors sticking way out in front and then a honking gap between those and their molars. The incisors have a chiseled edge that's sharpened by use. These grow continuously throughout life (as is the case with many rodents), and squirrels must wear them down.

Squirrels are also known for their tails. The tail becomes an effective blanket when it is cold, an umbrella when it is wet, and a cooling system when it is hot. In hot weather a squirrel can dilate arteries at the base of the tail to allow blood to rush down its length, where the heat from its core may dissipate.

The scientific name for the squirrel genus is *Sciurus,* which translates roughly to "shade-tail." The squirrels in North American cities are eastern grays (*Sciurus carolinensis,* "Carolina shade-tail") and eastern fox squirrels (*S. niger,* "swarthy shade-tail"). The eastern grays also come in black—as do many of those around Washington, DC—and there are a few populations that are entirely white.

Eastern grays were the first to populate cities, but fox squirrels, which are larger and have bigger brains, are pushing them out in some places, like my town. Fox squirrels have darker coats, with a ruddy orange fringe along the bottom by their paws.

Outside cities, there are several others: the western gray in the Sierra Nevada, the Arizona gray and Abert's squirrels in the Southwest, and the Eurasian red across the Atlantic. In England the red squirrels have retreated to the northern conifer forests because they are unable to cope with the diseases introduced by eastern grays—one native American species taking retribution for smallpox and cholera. In North America our conifer tree squirrels are larder hoarders that build and defend towers of cones. In the east there is the red squirrel, *Tamiasciurus hudsonicus,* the hoarding shade-tail of the Hudson, and in the Pacific Northwest the Douglas squirrel, *T. douglasii.* But if you see a tree squirrel in a city, it's almost certainly a fox squirrel or an eastern gray.

Reluctant Urbanites

Before 1840, cities were pretty much squirrelfree. The historian Etienne Benson has shown that it took painstaking effort to urbanize squirrels. City beautifiers released squirrels first in Philadelphia, then in Boston, and in New Haven, Connecticut. They provided the animals with food and nesting boxes. Children were encouraged to bring them nuts and cakes.

These days we generally discourage kids from feeding wild animals. We want our city wildlife to live parallel to us, never quite touching us. But back then, people wanted to civilize wildlife. Benson relates that George Perkins Marsh, often called the first American environmentalist, applauded the city squirrels, saying their tameness "was a foretaste of the rewards to be expected when man moderated his destructive behavior toward nature." In other words, once Americans stopped conquering the land, we could settle down to live in harmony with the conquered. That harmony would look a lot like a city park full of gracious trees and squirrels that would eat out of your hand.

And eat they did: A report in 1865 declared that the squirrels in New Haven Green had "become so obese from good living that they are continually missing their hold and falling from the tree tops." But despite all this effort to feed and house the rodents, the initial squirrel urbanization projects failed. The squirrels died; the environment just couldn't support them. Presumably, after the initial enthusiasm for feeding squirrels wore off, obesity gave way to starvation. To move in and take over cities, squirrels needed an ally to reshape their landscapes. They found that ally in Frederick Law Olmsted.

Olmsted introduced the idea that cities should contain large tracts of idealized wilderness (his most famous design was New York's Central Park). It was ideal for reading poetry in the shade or wandering with a friend, but mostly, it was ideal for being a squirrel.

In 1883, six years after sixty-eight squirrels were released in Central Park, it had an estimated population of 1,500. Olmsted is the acknowledged father of American landscape architecture, but it's not as well recognized that he also is the father of city squirrels. City dwellers unwittingly contributed to the effort by lining the streets with trees and installing elevated squirrel transportation infrastructure in the form of telephone and electrical lines.

To Love or to Kill

In the late 1800s, not everyone approved of Marsh's vision of wilderness tamed. There were also those who said it was ludicrous to think that nature could ever be conquered and wanted to keep fighting it. This debate was personified on one side by Ernest Thompson Seton, who in 1910 helped start the Boy Scouts of America and wanted to befriend nature. On the other side was Theodore Roosevelt, who wanted to hunt down and kill nature. Both Roosevelt and Seton were fascinated with manliness, and they both believed that communion with wild animals was a crucial part of the mystical process that transformed boys into men of character. But their agreement ended there.

Seton thought squirrels would teach boys to be nurturing and empathetic. "Some day," Seton wrote, "while a boy is feeding a squirrel, a dog may dash at it with evil design and the child will certainly and naturally try to save the squirrel that he was feeding, and thus cast in his lot with the squirrels against the dogs."

This would plant a seed of empathy that would blossom into righteousness and chivalry. Seton wrote, "You can rely on work being done by these missionary squirrels whose influence will not end with the boundaries of the city park, but will continue to go as far as the boys go."

Roosevelt thought squirrels, and all wild animals, were there to teach boys to learn courage. In his view, you'd start by killing spiders and beetles, move on to birds and squirrels, work your way up to bears, and before you know it you'd be a general like him. Ultimately, you'd need a war to truly become a man, and Roosevelt lamented that too much peace was emasculating the United States. Instead of teaching boys to protect squirrels so that they might later protect people, Roosevelt wanted boys to kill squirrels so they might later kill people.

Roosevelt attacked Seton for being a "nature faker," and the slur stuck because it was true, at least in part. Seton sought to teach morality with animals, but to do this he took outrageous liberties in giving animals human qualities, populating his writing with heroic rabbits, crows that fly in military formation, and rams driven by dandyish pride.

But Roosevelt was just as much a faker. He constructed his macho persona from the ground up. When he first entered public life at the age of twenty-three as a New York state assemblyman, he was a rich kid with soft hands, a squeaky voice, and clothes that were a little too fashionable for his own good. The newspapers gave him nicknames: "Jane-Dandy," "our own Oscar Wilde," and "Punkin-Lily." He went west to shake this reputation. Viewed from this angle, Roosevelt's entire life looks like one gigantic exercise in overcompensation.

This argument between Roosevelt and Seton over nature and manhood had staying power. To this day, when people argue about saving endangered species or managing wildfires or responding to climate change, you can detect the ghosts of Roosevelt and Seton in the background.

I've spent a lot of time considering what lessons I want to pass on to my own kids. I grew up in the Seton mode: I understood that my moral development depended on protecting squirrels rather than shooting them. And yet, I wouldn't want to pass on Seton's ideology to Josephine, because it has so little grounding in reality. I'd also like to keep her away from Rooseveltian displays of masculine violence. Rather than conquering nature or giving it fake human morality, I'd want her to simply approach nature with open eyes and curiosity.

The Squirrel That Owns My House

One of the benefits of writing about squirrels, as opposed to, say, wolves, is that—thanks to those nineteenth-century civic boosters—you can see them without any effort. There's one squirrel that likes to eat the rose hips that hang over our wooden fence. It's a fox squirrel, orange and white underneath and gray on his back. One morning he and I found ourselves face-to-face as I was taking my coffee grounds out to the compost pile. The squirrel was on top of the fence, at eye level about three feet away, gripping a rose hip in his mouth. There was what seemed like an insane intensity in his beady, close-set eyes. He regarded me with a cheeky lack of respect, then scrabbled forward and down onto the vertical face of the fence, all four legs spread. In this gravity-defying position, he traversed to the far end of my backyard.

I can't help but see human emotions in squirrels. But I try not to go as far as Seton did—I refrain from making up motives and morals, and I strive to watch closely enough that my ideas might be shattered by something a squirrel does.

I don't feel bad about anthropomorphizing my furry neighbor. That's just how people work: We project our own expectations and ways of understanding the world onto the creatures around us, be they squirrels or family members. A few days earlier Josephine—at this point three years old, and a genius—had seen the same squirrel running along the same fence.

"Papa," she said, pointing. "A cat!"

I do the same thing; I just don't have someone around to correct me. We see what we expect to, what we have a name for, what pops immediately into our heads. But confirmation of the expected is boring, and false. Life only becomes interesting when you watch it closely enough to see something surprising, and with that surprise come a little closer to the real thing. That,

I suppose, is the point of this book: to allow people to see past their expectations. When *actual seeing* pierces the skin of habituation, if only for a moment, it permits a bit of wonder to bleed through. Wonder is the animating ether that allows some lucky few to perceive not just the prosaic, but the most profound laws of the universe at work in the prosaic. I think that's what the poet Philip Appleman was getting at in the prologue of *Darwin's Bestiary* when he wrote:

> *The habit stays with us, albeit it's puerile:*
> *when Darwin saw squirrels, he saw more than*
> *Squirrel.*

SQUIRRELS ON SQUIRRELS

I think the hardest part of squirrel life, at least for the males, must be finding a mate. That's because there are between five and twenty male squirrels for every female. Moreover, that one female is only receptive to males twice a year for a few hours at a time. The males go into a fevered mania during that breeding period, monitoring the females and then joining in daylong contests for their affections. Researchers have seen as many as thirty-three males participating in these competitions. These mating bouts look, Koprowski and Steele write, like "pure and unadulterated chaos."

The males fight each other for position, often doing serious damage with their powerful incisors and sharp claws. The dominant male then advances on the female. But the female usually has her own ideas and sprints away. The males give chase in single file. If they lose track of her, mayhem descends. They dash back and forth across the female's territory, chirping in what sounds like a high-pitched sneeze. They will chase, with amorous intent, anything that moves. Researchers have seen frenzied males pursue blue jays, rabbits, crows, and, once, a softball.

A female may initiate these chases for her own safety, because it's dangerous to mate in front of a lust-crazed mob. Attackers disrupt 20 percent of mating attempts, sometimes knocking the pair out of the tree. Usually the female stops in a safe location (i.e., close to the ground) and mates with the first male to reach her after a chase. If she's managed to outrun them all, she calls out until a male finds her. The male guards the female for about twenty minutes after mating, but then the maneuvers begin again, and the whole circus can recur several times before the end of the day.

The fall breeding season is hard on males. They come out the other side injured and skinny. As Steele and Koprowski write, "Nothing demonstrated this to us more graphically than when we watched a rather groggy adult male fox squirrel emerge in the early morning hours and fall dead to the ground. Upon conducting a necropsy of this individual, we observed that he had 14 wounds from other squirrels and no visible body fat stores. He died primarily of malnutrition."

And yet, this sad specimen was a winner: He had copulated five times that breeding season.

The Domestic Squirrel

Squirrel life isn't always so competitive. They also cooperate. Eastern gray squirrels may live together in groups of two to nine, cuddling up in big leafy nests and grooming each other when they emerge in the morning. When it's a group of females, they are usually related, and they keep coming back night after night—there's an evolutionary benefit in taking care of someone when you share genes. The male groups aren't as stable, but they are even more remarkable because they nest with compatriots that aren't closely related. They are able to form alliances with other bachelors without the force of family.

The nests are properly called dreys. When Jo and I went looking for acorns we were looking down at first, searching the ground. But then, while under a big tree, I looked up. The leaves formed a thick layer of green around the farthest extent of the tree, but the interior stems of a coast live oak are bare. Looking up the trunk was like looking into the complicated mechanism of a massive green umbrella. I could clearly see a drey straddling two branches.

"Look, Josephine, do you want to see a squirrel house?"

She dropped the pinecone she'd been picking at and trotted over. "Where?"

I crouched next to her and pointed. "It looks like a big ball of leaves. See it?"

Jo laughed in her low, huffy chortle, which signifies deep satisfaction.

But even as I was pointing, I saw another, smaller drey, and then another, and another. Dreys are a perfect example of the unseen city: Even if you think you've never seen them before, you probably have—anywhere there are squirrels, there are dreys, hiding in plain sight. But they are easy to miss because they look so messy, like a mass of leaves lodged high in the tree. But masses of leaves don't just lodge in trees. That takes intention.

Squirrels start by building a base of leafy forked branches, then pile twigs atop that until it's at least a foot across. Then, according to squirrel researchers Monica Shorten and Frederick Barkalow Jr., they will "dive and wiggle into the middle of the heap, using hands and mouth to tug and bite, and, judging by what can be seen from a distance, the cavity is shaped by repeated body turns."

After lining the interior with moss, leaves, shredded bark, and whatever else is handy, the squirrel has a waterproof home with an interior of about the size of a bocce ball, on average. Obviously the drey must be bigger for a larger group.

The entrance to a drey is always covered by leaves, but you can see squirrels coming or leaving if you are willing to spend some time waiting. Just before sunset is a good time to set up watch: That's when they return to their homes. But unless you are up in the canopy, it's hard to tell which squirrel is going into which drey. As we were looking up into the live oak's branches, a squirrel materialized and clambered toward us.

"Does he live in that nest?" Jo asked.

I had no clue; he could have been lurking in the upper branches, so I answered with another question. "Maybe, but Josephine, how do you know it's not a girl?"

"Because, Papa," she said, laughing at my ignorance, "he's not wearing earrings."

Here's how you determine the sex of a squirrel: Wait until it stands on its hind legs, and then look for nipples or testicles. Josephine was right about this particular squirrel—it was almost certainly a male, because it had no nipples. If you look closely, they are clearly visible, unless the female is less than a year old and hasn't had babies yet. The males are trickier: They have pendulous scrotums, but they retract into their bodies during July and August, between mating seasons (in eastern gray squirrels).

Learning to recognize individuals is an important step in becoming a good field observer of squirrels, the researchers say, and learning to see which are males and females helps with that. Then you can begin to look for more subtle details, such as variations in color, patterns, or scars.

Individuals can also be identified by their behavior. The morning after we found the dreys, Josephine pointed out that our backyard squirrel had joined us for breakfast. It was perched on the fence a few feet from the dining room window, eating rose hips. I was sure it was the same squirrel, not because I could see any identifying marks, but because of the rose hips and his manner. Just as before, he was fervently unafraid. He continued shelling the pulp off the rose hips, then cracking the seeds inside, even when I opened the window and Josephine leaned out over the sill, not five feet away.

He returned the next day during breakfast, and the next. There was no doubt that it was the same squirrel. After finishing each rose hip he paused to wipe his short muzzle against the fence, first one side, then the other. He steadily depleted the supply of rose hips, clambering farther out into the hanging brambles to procure those he couldn't reach from the fence. His movements were not particularly graceful. Twice I saw him fall, but he always caught himself immediately. Perhaps squirrels favor resilience over precision: Instead of calculating each movement like a rock climber, they just scramble forward and trust in their strong claws if a foothold fails.

After a week, there were no more easily accessible rose hips. There was one branch laden with red fruit, but it extended too precariously for our squirrel. He tested his weight on it and then retreated to eat the black rose hips of years past instead.

I picked one of the fresh rose hips to see what our squirrel was after. Inside were eleven slick seeds, each about the size and shape of a lemon seed. They were tremendously difficult to crack, and each time I succeeded in breaking through the husk with a knife, the pieces scattered across the kitchen. The black rose hips I picked contained only a couple of fat seeds, the rest being withered and thin. I picked a few of the fresh rose hips from the forbidden bough and left them along the top of the fence to see if our neighbor would take them, or if he now preferred the older vintage.

The next day my offering was reduced to bits. I replaced it with several more rose hips, but these remained untouched atop my fence. Another puzzle. The squirrels gave me a clue the next morning. Often, I'll hear squirrels—their claws on bark, or a tumult of clattering branches—before I see them. As I sat on the stoop lacing my running shoes, I became aware that there were at least two squirrels in the oak tree across the street. One bounded directly at me, and when it reached my front yard I could see that it held an acorn in its mouth. Perhaps the acorns had ripened and rose hips were suddenly passé.

The squirrel buried the nut and I kept my gaze fixed on the tuft of grass that marked the spot. Koprowski and Steele had written that "ultimately, the squirrels' decision of what to eat and what to cache may determine the structure, composition, and population biology of our oak forests." I would add that it's not only our forests, but also our yards, medians, and city parks. I'd noticed two small sprouts emerging from the earth beside our house, both of them coast live oaks, and I realized it was entirely possible that this very squirrel had planted them. There was news breaking in my neighborhood that was going unreported: news of the squirrels' plans for the long-term development of the urban forest, news of acorns ripening and the relative size of the year's crop, news of the way the replacement of the eastern grays by fox squirrels had changed the rhythms of these cycles within cycles. I could see just enough to see what I was missing. I crossed the sidewalk and resolutely excavated the turf where I'd seen the squirrel bury the acorn. It was nowhere to be found.

BIRD
LANGUAGE

ONE MORNING, AFTER JOSEPHINE HAD talked her way into our bed—then spent the rest of the night rotating through a series of improbable sleeping positions—as we lay clinging to the last shreds of sleep, she asked why the birds were singing so loudly. I've grown so accustomed to the morning chorus of birds outside our window that I hadn't noticed, but yes, they were rather loud.

"What are they saying?" she asked. "Why are they all *tweet-twee-tweet*?"

I considered this. Was there an answer to this question? Why do birds wake so early to talk to one another? And was it possible to divine the meaning of their songs?

There are scientists who think that birds sing at first light to signal that they have survived the night and are laying claim to their territory for another day. Others suggest that they sing in the time after waking when it's still too dark to forage. I think both of these hypotheses can be combined with the one I find most compelling: They hash out their territorial rights when

they first wake up, because it's the time when there's the least
competition for the acoustic airspace. As I was researching this
question I stumbled upon the story of the Talbots, a family living in southwest England, that demonstrated the point. I found
and friended Ali Talbot on Facebook. A few days later I was
chatting on the phone with her husband, Nathan. He laid out
the story for me.

Every morning at 5:00 a.m., they would hear the siren. The
Talbots live near a hospital, so sirens aren't unusual, but this one
was peculiar. Instead of sweeping by, it stayed put, as if the
source was parked in their backyard. "The hospital is about half
a mile from my house, so at first I thought it was an ambu-
lance," Nathan Talbot told me. "It woke me up every single day
at 5:00 a.m. It was uncanny! It was like an alarm clock." It
cycled through the typical phases, sometimes stopping just long
enough to make them think it was finished before starting again.
And it happened every morning at the same time. Sometimes it
would sound like the ringtone of a cell phone that never went to
voicemail. Sometimes it sounded just like a car alarm. But there
was something strange about it: Though the volume was just as
jarring as sirens normally are, the timbre was slightly higher and
thinner, more of a whistle than a siren. Eventually Nathan went
out into his garden and sighted the culprit: a blackbird. It was
perched right above his dormer window.

Wild birds all over the world have changed their tunes as the
noises associated with people dominate cities. Most of these
changes don't involve mimicry—the blackbird in the Talbots'
yard was exceptional. Instead, birds are shifting their songs in
order to compete with humanity's hubbub, so they can be heard.

In places where the morning commute creates tumult, birds have set their alarms earlier: Long before first light, they sing to declare the boundaries of their territories. If shifting their schedule is impractical, birds sometimes shift pitch instead, adjusting their vocal register up or down so they aren't in competition with the buzz of engines.

One of the first people to realize that animals were listening to the songs of other species and adjusting their own songs to accommodate them was Bernie Krause, a musician turned natural-sound engineer. Krause was recording in Kenya's Maasai Mara National Reserve when he had his epiphany. It was hours after midnight, and he was listening to the sounds of the reserves while drifting between wakefulness and sleep. "It was in that semifloating state—that transition between the blissful suspension of awareness and the depths of total unconsciousness—that I first encountered the transparent weave of creature voices not only as a choir but as a cohesive sonic event," Krause wrote in his book *The Great Animal Orchestra*. "No longer a cacophony, it became a partitioned collection of vocal organisms—a highly orchestrated acoustic arrangement of insects, spotted hyenas, eagle-owls, African wood-owls, elephants, tree hyrax, distant lions, and several knots of tree frogs and toads. Every distinct voice seemed to fit within its own acoustic bandwidth."

Put simply, each creature was filling a special place in the sonic spectrum, some of them the higher registers, others the lower. If this were a visual phenomenon rather than auditory, every species' song would have been a different color of the rainbow, each one stacked above the next. When Krause printed out a visual spectrogram of his recording, it looked to him like musical notation: Each animal fit into its own track, where it wouldn't overlap with and be muddied by the sounds of another. In a very real way, the animals were an orchestra: Each instrument made itself heard by producing a different set of frequencies. The elephants were the bass cellos, the hyenas the oboes, the hyraxes the clarinets, the insects the violins, and the bats the piccolos over the top.

In cities, however, a constant wash of mechanical noise fills a massive swath of the audio spectrum. Birds have adjusted, but there's only so much they can change in what is in evolutionary terms—a short period of time. House sparrows are declining in some areas because, scientists suspect, they can't communicate with one another. Some species of bat, which rely on echolocation to hunt, have moved out of noisy areas. And, of course, the problem isn't limited to cities: Ship engine noise and the other sounds people make in the oceans can have deleterious effects on dolphins and whales.

All the noise is bad for animals, and for us. Constant exposure to mechanical noise is unpleasant, and there's some evidence that it can chronically elevate stress and erode our health. One of its gravest effects may be the separation of humans from the orchestra of life. We'd be much more likely to quiet down if we were interested in listening to what our nonhuman neighbors were telling us—that is, if we all learned to speak the language of birds.

SONGS WITHOUT LYRICS

It turns out that learning to understand the bird language doesn't require a magical amulet or an enchanted silver seashell, but instead something that's arguably more difficult to come by: patience. When I picked up Jon Young's book *What the Robin Knows,* I was a little worried I was about to waste my time trying to acquire occult knowledge. But as I read, I became impressed by the modesty of Young's claims. He states the facts without embellishment, and offers a skill for the price of forced concentration.

I'd thought I'd start learning to identify birds by their songs, but Young admits that is sometimes impossible. He writes, "Even aces can have trouble identifying a new species on the basis of song alone." Songs vary across the country, and across the yard. A Bewick's wren may sing different songs than its father does a few hundred yards away. Instead of obsessing over species identification, Young focuses on the salient landmarks in bird dialect, and on the way they correlate with behavior. He doesn't try to recognize and read each trill and semiquaver for literal meaning. Instead, Young listens for the emotion and the intent behind the song. You've already done this, he points out, if you've ever listened to someone singing in a language you don't understand: "Listening to Spanish, Italian, or German opera, you, like me, may have no idea what the words of a particular aria mean, but you don't need this knowledge to understand the feeling they convey. You can tell if it's a song of pleasure, jubilation, triumph, or tragedy."

I found that if I focused on the birdsong, I could easily hear singing and scolding and—perhaps the most revealing soundscape of all—silence. While reading Young's book I couldn't help but begin to notice the bird noises outside my window: peeps and chirps. It was a warm winter day, so I went out to the backyard to sit in the sun. As I was reading, monitoring the birdsong around me with a sliver of my attention, the chirping ceased. It was a subtle change, one I wouldn't have noticed normally. The other sounds still continued, of course—the cars passing, the shouts of children at the nearby playground—but the underlying fabric of birdsong had disappeared, like a tablecloth whisked away from under the place settings with such delicacy that I would have missed it if I hadn't been listening for it. I climbed the steps to my back door and stood on my toes to look over the fence. There were about a dozen students walking east on the greenway that borders my house. They were holding hands, forming a cordon that swept across the park. I felt a little shiver of triumph. The birds had told me that something was happening, and I had been ready to hear.

How to Hear Birds

Young's method for learning bird language is simple: Find a spot and go there every day to watch and listen to birds. Though I had experienced my first triumph on that winter morning, I had actually been doing it wrong. First, I was reading, rather than giving my full attention to the birds, and second, my backyard is barely big enough for one little raised vegetable bed, and a high wooden fence surrounds it. I could hear the birds, but I couldn't see them, so I couldn't connect sounds to behavior.

As you learn bird language, a new world is supposed to open up to you. Young tells the story of a teenager he calls Jack, who immediately tired of the lessons. After sitting alone in his spot, Jack told Young that there weren't any birds around. But over the course of the school year, Young writes:

"no birds" became "a few birds," which morphed into "some little brown noisy birds," then into "flocks of little black and white ones that stayed in the trees" and "other birds I couldn't really see." One day Jack announced he had seen "some Pacific wrens" (those "little brown noisy birds") and some "chickadees in the trees" (those "little black and white ones"). . . . Then "the Pacific wren seemed upset because another Pacific wren came close to this one's favorite stump."

In one sense this was a modest change: Jack learned the names of a couple of species and came to understand what they were doing. But in another sense, he gained a superpower. He went from not seeing anything to recognizing individual birds and perceiving the invisible outlines of their territories. This isn't useful by the normal measures of humans—it's not going to make Jack money or get him a girlfriend—but it does provide a sense of a place. What's true of other people is also true of places: to know deeply is to love more. To know the secrets of a place, to read it on many levels, and to sense the vastness of the unknown is, I think, the key to love.

Failing at Bird-Watching

It was a cool February morning, still damp with dew. Brown birds were hopping around under the live oaks across the street. I sat on my stoop doing my time, watching as Young had instructed. I felt good. This seemed like the right way to learn birdsongs: Observe the birds and connect them to their songs naturally. It was much more doable than trying to memorize a series of notes from a recording.

While I watched, a pair of birds foraging on my neighbor's driveway protested in mild distress and surged upward, into the trees. They might been frightened by a predator, but I hadn't seen enough to feel the slightest confidence in that conclusion. In the dense canopy of one oak, a bird was chirping more and more loudly, like a parent yelling at a toddler who isn't listening. But I had no clue what was going on.

There was birdsong all around me, but which birds were producing it? A pair of black dots flitted across the sky and were gone. Birds, I assumed.

I took off my glasses and rubbed my eyes. *Maybe I need to get binoculars,* I thought, but what would my neighbors think if they saw me sitting on my stoop, scanning our tiny street with binoculars?

Hearing the Future

Spend enough time studying bird language, Young writes, and you'll be freaking out your friends by announcing that a cat is coming just before it appears.

"Birds have always been messengers," Young says. "They've always brought us messages about the safety of the land around us."

There's nothing mystical about this: birds are just always spewing out information. They create a sort of sonic Internet. All sorts of animals tune in to this exchange of data, alert for ripples of disturbance, sometimes adding their own contributions, sometimes manipulating the chatter in their own favor.

Young identifies five types of bird noises: baseline songs,

companion calls, territorial squabbles, juvenile begging, and alarms. When I began sitting and watching birds, I heard mostly companion calls, with songs and the occasional alarm thrown in. Companion calls are simple chirps back and forth ("You good?" "Yep. You?"). I wasn't hearing many songs, I think, because it was still winter, too early for nesting. Songs generally advertise the boundaries of territories, those three-dimensional spaces individual birds claim as their own. When these property lines are well established, Young writes, you can see an obvious change when a bird crosses over. A robin that is cocky on his own turf will become furtive when he slips into a neighbor's property.

Of all the signals the birds were sending, the alarms were the most interesting to me because they indicated the detection of something beyond my visual field. The shape of a disturbance often allows an experienced bird interpreter to decipher what sort of creature is triggering an alert. A predator on the wing creates a "wave of alarms, followed by a tunnel of silence," Young writes. A strolling cat causes birds to "hook" up to a slightly higher perch while also broadcasting a mild alarm. A human blundering through acts as a "bird plow," oblivious to all they are flushing out of their path.

Young tells one story of watching Pacific wrens sound the alarm as something moved through a salmonberry thicket near his house outside Seattle: The birds would scold vigorously, then stop, peer into the bushes, and scold again. Young concluded that there was a weasel among the salmonberries, disappearing and then reappearing in another spot. This is a classic weasel pattern. Weasels are elusive predators that can vanish into rodent holes and slip beneath dead sticks and leaves, only to pop up in a new place.

Young had just moved from New Jersey, so he asked a local who helped take care of the land if there were weasels around. The man assured him there were not. Young was puzzled, until he began to find other indisputable signs: road-killed weasels, and a nest of baby weasels in a Volkswagen behind his house. The weasels were there all right, they were just too sneaky for human eyes. But Young could see them through the birds.

LOOK SMART

I was having trouble seeing the birds at all, let alone detecting more stealthy beasts from their movements. I swallowed my sense of neighborly decorum and, one Sunday, took Josephine to a sporting goods store to buy a pair of binoculars. I found some I liked for just under $100; they had the right magnification, but not all the high-tech materials. As soon as we got home Josephine insisted that she should have right to their exclusive use. I tightened the strap around her neck and made her promise to be careful with them, and to keep her fingers off the lenses. They were comically large when she pressed them to her little face. She gazed at the sky, at her feet, at the trees, and then she turned the binoculars around the wrong way and repeated the sequence.

I got my chance to use the binoculars after leaving Josephine at daycare the next day. It took me a while to master the focusing wheel, but once I did, I began seeing birds with remarkable clarity. The sun was fiercely bright and a little black bird was swooping toward the grass, then back up into the trees. It would perch, then swoop down, making acrobatic midair turns. Through the binoculars I could see this bird was dressed in a tuxedo and a starched white shirt, with fluffy feathers on its black head. When I went to the Cornell Lab of Ornithology's Bird Guide Web site, I spotted it right away: a black phoebe. It's a fly-catching bird, which explains the acrobatics. I felt momentarily triumphant, but overall I was frustrated. This bird-watching thing was hard, harder than watching snails or trees, I mused resentfully.

That night I called up Mike Nelson, a friend of my brother's and an amateur naturalist who had offered to give me pointers. He assured me that I wasn't going blind, and that binoculars really are helpful, even for birds just across the street. As a kid, he told me, he had a very short list of the birds he'd seen until he got binoculars. Then, he said, "all of a sudden I was like, 'Holy crap, I just found six more species, all in my backyard.'"

Mike also told me to stop beating myself up over failing to connect songs to specific birds. Just watching and listening probably wouldn't do the trick, he said, because I'd also be surrounded by the songs of unseen birds. And he thought learning from a book would be just as hard: "If you try and read about it in a guidebook, it will say something like, '*twitch-twitch-twitch* rising on the third note and then alternating with a wheezy buzz.' Good luck remembering that!" The way to do it, he said, was to hang out with someone who knew the sounds and let that person teach me.

His method was to listen to the birdsongs and link them to a story or image as a mnemonic. "So a wrentit, for instance, is

like a lifeguard getting progressively more angry, blowing on its
whistle. Or there's the common yellowthroat, which has a call
that sounds like *whichisit-whichisit*. It's yellow with what looks
a little like a black mask, so I imagine that it's a frightened thief
running into a museum and trying to figure out what to steal:
whichisit-whichisit-whichisit!"

Mike suggested I learn a few of the most common birds first
to get my bearings, and promised to send me a list.

I'd love to be able to recognize every bird by its song (Mike
knows them well enough to stop whenever he hears something
he *doesn't* recognize), but I'd settle for simply having a better
grasp of my surroundings. I'd like push notifications on my
phone that tell me when each bird arrives in spring, and how
they are doing with nesting and finding food. Bird language provides those notifications—it's the original social network.
Young uses a different metaphor: "Nervousness among robins
flocking in the winter," Young writes, "is a great barometer of
neighborhood tension." If I can't have notifications, a barometer
will do just fine.

The most basic readings from this barometer tell a story of
lucky coincidence and adaptation. The most common birds we
see today are the ones that found they could thrive in the environments humans created. Nighthawks nest on gravel rooftops
and chimney swifts rely on human-made structures (notably
chimneys), while house sparrows nest under eaves. Mown lawns
produce an earthworm buffet for crows and robins, and house
sparrows travel to highway rest stops to eat the bugs splattered
on car windshields.

BIRDSONG AND MENTAL HEALTH

Young is careful to talk about birds that live near people, like robins and house finches and song sparrows. He suggests finding an observation spot that's immediately at hand—certainly not a place you have to drive to, and ideally one that's no more than a few minutes' walk away. There's no need to seek out untouched wilderness, because the bird closest at hand is the best teacher. And a city bird teaches more than its language.

Often when I'm working, I'll have several windows open on my computer at once: I'm chatting with half a dozen colleagues in one window and monitoring what people are saying about my latest piece on another, while also responding to e-mails and fielding phone calls. Sometimes my mind snaps under all this stimulation and I enter a sort of fugue state in which I manically click from one window to another without accomplishing anything. It's hard to break out of this; the feeling is remarkably similar to the sense of being powerless to stop eating spoonful after spoonful of ice cream.

But I've found that spending five minutes watching birds on my front stoop is a reliable cure for this frenzy. I come away calmer. I think more clearly afterward. I suspect this is because watching the birds allows me to exercise a very different part of my brain. Instead of receiving hundreds of digital jolts coming in from the outside, all specifically directed at *me, me, me!*, I'm reaching outward. I'm trying to empathize with another species, understand their culture. Instead of being at the focal point of a million strands of information, I am an outsider trying to connect. This not only feels healthy, it also feels more honest than my online existence. There's much more to life than existing as a node in the information web.

It's not that nature doesn't send the equivalent of status updates directly to me, it's that normally I'm just oblivious to them. I'm only just beginning to notice when it's *me* the birds are talking about. Whenever I tune in to bird language, I begin to feel the reality of interdependence. It's like a chiropractic adjustment for the brain.

As promised, Mike sent me a list of birds to learn. I had been expecting a literal list of names, but instead he created a multi-media document with photos, recordings of songs, and his favorite factoids. Anna's hummingbirds steal insects from spiders and use their webs "to hold their shot-glass-sized nests together." House finches, whose red-tinted heads I'd just learned to see, have a jumbled warble that often ends "with an upward slur, which makes them sound like they are saying: *blah-blah-blah-blah-blah-RIGHT?*" Some of the hidden birds I'd heard singing in the bushes turned out to be hermit thrushes, furtive relatives of robins. And you can identify a robin's song, Mike wrote, by listening for a cadence that sounds like *cheerily–cheer up–cheer up–cheerily–cheer up.*

I was learning, but slowly. I'd figure out the names of half a dozen birds on one day, only to forget them the next. Josephine, curiously, was much better at remembering names than I was.

"What is that bird?" I'd ask. "With the white stripe over its eye and the upturned tail?"

"Um, is it a Bewick's wren?" she'd answer, correctly.

The decline in my powers of retention was distressing, but

predicable. The young mind is calibrated for absorption: Josephine was learning new words every day, so it's no surprise that
she could learn birds. Mike also had started learning young. At
my age, without extraordinary effort, I might never become flu-
ent in bird language. Josephine has the chance, but not necessarily the inclination. She's curious about birds, but she's much
more curious about ballerinas. That's fine with me: I just want
her to have the opportunity.

Birdsong is just one of the millions of signals that most
humans ignore on a regular basis. We can't pay attention to
everything—that would be maddening—so we pick and choose.
But the point is that often we don't choose: We listen, by default,
to the voices in our heads rather than the voices of our avian
neighbors. I find that I'm happier when I listen to the world
rather than to the whining of my doubts.

If we started listening to birds, perhaps we'd get a little qui-
eter (it's hard to listen while making noise) in ways that would
benefit both birds and humans. We'd probably be both happier
and healthier. But even more interesting, in my view, is that we'd
begin to perceive an unseen world of gossip and warfare and
love all around us. And if we understood this language, I think
we'd make different choices: not to stop building and living, but
just to be a little more thoughtful in the way that we live.

GINKGO

IN THE FIRST AUTUMN AFTER we moved from San Francisco to Berkeley, I would regularly walk from my house to the university campus in the mornings. Every time I made this journey, at about the halfway point, I'd find myself in a state of high dudgeon. This agitation invariably struck just before I reached Shattuck Avenue. The world grew unpardonable. Whatever I happened to be thinking about—some argument with a critic online, some puzzle in my writing, some exchange with Josephine— would turn over in my brain until it itched with offensive implications. The warmth of the sun, the crispness of the air, the students cycling past, all were loaded with insult. I was like a character in a Dostoyevsky novel, suddenly livid for no apparent reason.

Then I would cross Shattuck and my world would steady on its axis. I'd notice that I was walking on a typically beautiful fall day, on a street lined with gold-leaved trees. I'd remember how grateful I am to have work and a family that I love.

I wasn't fully conscious of this bizarre mood swing at first. But one day, I set out on my walk with the suspicion that there was something about that particular block that set me awry.

This time, it was about as subtle as an air horn braying at my head. After I crossed the street, this silent air horn disappeared as quickly as it had started up. It was like I received a powerful mood-altering injection that wore off after precisely one block— and always the same block. I stopped and walked back. Why was I so annoyed? It was only then that I became aware of the stench. Occasional breaths of rot, wisps of vomit, wafted delicately in the breeze.

Smell is the most subliminal of the senses. Volatile chemicals can slip into our sensory receptors and work powerful magic on our emotions, without alerting us to their presence. It may be different for sommeliers, but I suspect that the Proustian effect of smell on emotion is related to the fact that scents act below the level of consciousness.

I looked up and immediately guessed the source. Those beautiful gold leaves clung to the limbs of ginkgo trees, and their seeds were underfoot. They were each about an inch in diameter and covered in desiccating flesh, like greasy yellow dates. They were putrefying with fury.

I'd only recently learned that ginkgos produce stinky seeds, but had assumed that the friend who mentioned their smell was just supremely sensitive. I'd never noticed that the trees smelled bad, and I'd never seen the seeds.

Most trees are hermaphrodites. Each oak tree, for instance, produces both acorns (female) and pollen-spreading catkins (male). Each pine makes both pinecones and pollen cones. But ginkgos have distinct males and females. Because ginkgo seeds smell so bad, people often plant only the males. This is true for other trees as well: Yews, ash, holly, junipers, poplars, and willows all come in male and female varieties. Landscapers and city arborists often favor the males so there will be less fruit and other reproductive equipment falling from the branches. But by choosing males, we are also opting for pollen. A big male ginkgo can throw a trillion rugby-ball-shaped grains of pollen into the air every spring.

This trade-off between spring pollen and autumn stench made me wonder: What are we doing planting ginkgos in the first place? Why populate our cities with these particular trees? And, on the other side, what were ginkgos "thinking" when they evolved to produce such offensive fruit? Clearly they weren't considering human sensibilities. But who, then, is the ginkgo seed designed to titillate?

THE SURVIVOR

Is there any leaf as strange as the *Ginkgo biloba*? Most tree leaves are built around a main backbone running up the middle with ribs branching off to each side. The structure of ginkgo's dual-lobed fan (the source of the name "biloba") is strangely simple: The veins run from the edge of the leaf all the way down its stem. Sometimes they divide in two, but they never resemble the normal branching networks. If we were built the same way, a capillary in your little finger would run directly back to your heart rather than connecting to a nearby artery. In fact, the ginkgo's leaf design is unique among seed-bearing plants.

Some hundred million years ago, leaves like this shaded dinosaurs on every continent. The ginkgo trees that grow in our towns are virtually identical to the ginkgos that began to appear two hundred million years ago. The golden age of the ginkgo family, Ginkgophyta (technically a whole division of plant life), was the Cretaceous, which lasted from 140 million to 80 million years ago.

Evolutionarily, Ginkgophytes are between ferns and modern flowering plants. The pollen of almost every other plant is passive: It floats around, and if any grain ends up in just the right place, in just the right flower, it can deliver its payload of genes. Ginkgo pollen, by contrast, is active: Once it lands on a female plant's seed cone, it opens up and releases sperm that swim using their thousands of filaments arranged in spirals. I find it astounding that something so stationary (a tree!) can produce a mobile creature that rides the wind out into the world and then scrambles to the finish line to spread its DNA. Imagine if evolution had scaled this up and trees made little walking body parts to carry and bury their seeds.

Ginkgophytes thrived in a warmer, wetter time, when the poles were temperate regions and now-extinct monsters browsed among the trees. As botanist Peter Crane puts it in his book *Ginkgo*, "Several different kinds of ginkgolike trees watched as our ancestors transformed from reptiles to mammals." Perhaps those scuttling ancestors chewed ginkgo fruits. Something must have given the ginkgo a reason to produce those awful smells— some Cretaceous scavenger sniffing for decaying flesh.

The Ginkgophytes couldn't keep up with the changing planet. The world transformed dramatically sixty-five million years ago, when an asteroid slammed into what is now the Yucatán peninsula. The debris it threw into the atmosphere blocked the sun, making Earth colder. The dinosaurs died, and so did many relatives of the ginkgo. The Oligocene was rough for ginkgos too, and they disappeared from the poles. In the Miocene, they abandoned North America, and then died out in Europe during the Pliocene. Finally, after every one of the tree's relatives died off, only a few protected valleys in China harbored ginkgos. If we were similarly orphaned, it would mean that the planet would have lost all the creatures in which we see some flicker of commonality: all apes and monkeys, all dogs and whales and bears, all the rest of the mammals, all frogs and lizards and birds—all the creatures having a central nerve cord like our spinal cord, including many invertebrates, like sea squirts. Our closest remaining relatives would be things like starfish. If you can imagine a world in which we were the sole living representative of the phylum Chordata, then you can understand the isolation of the ginkgo.

It's tough for anachronisms like this to survive, because the symbiotic alliances they've made (such as the one oaks have made with squirrels) fall apart as their friends go extinct. But ginkgos managed to find a new friend: humans. The trees probably would have died off if people hadn't taken a liking to them. People have been nurturing ginkgos for at least two thousand years.

Humans carried the ginkgo out into the world, reversing its retreat. In 1730, Dutch merchants brought a ginkgo from Japan to the Botanic Garden in Utrecht, Holland. People were eager to plant this unusual tree. From there, the species traveled to England, and then, in 1784, to Philadelphia.

It seemed there was no place for the Ginkophytes as the age of dinosaurs became the age of mammals. But now, oddly, ginkgos find themselves uniquely suited to the age of humans. They are resistant to pollution and disease, and are famously resilient in the face of urban abuses (a ginkgo less then a kilometer from ground zero survived the nuclear blast at Hiroshima, though the shrine behind it was flattened). They prosper in the sticky heat of New Orleans and the cold winters of Montreal. They prefer good soil, but can grow well in a square of dirt between concrete slabs. They thrive in partial shade, which is what you get in the presence of tall buildings. By clinging to life for millions of years, these trees have landed in an era offering a new ecological niche—the city—for which they are perfectly adapted.

The Evolutionary Fingerprint of a Mystery Animal

The most compelling hypothesis I've seen to explain the decline of the Ginkgophytes is that the trees lost their seed distributors.

Many plants rely on partners of other species to help them reproduce: Darwin's orchid, for example, cannot complete the sex act without the cooperation of Morgan's sphinx moth and its twelve-inch-long tongue, which is precisely adapted to the shape of the flower. If one dies out, so will the other. Seed distributors are not quite so vital, and ginkgos can still reproduce quite well on their own. But without assistance, the trees only spread to new areas slowly. Each generation can travel only as far as a nut can roll. It takes thirty years for a ginkgo to reach sexual maturity and produce its first seed. So, about a foot per decade—far too slow to outrun glaciers. Plants often solve this problem by recruiting animals to carry their seeds.

Surely those pungent seeds evolved for a reason, besides annoying me. Ginkgos likely coated their seeds with stinking flesh to appeal to the sorts of creatures that love vile, stinking things. Perhaps it was a dinosaur or an ancient mammal that gravitated toward the smell of rotting meat. When this mystery creature ate the seeds, it would have absorbed the fruity exterior as it passed through its digestive system, but it would have deposited the seed itself, along with a small pile of fertilizing manure, in a new location. Ginkgo seeds sprout more readily if the fruit around them is removed.

This hypothesis is buttressed by the fact that several modern creatures eat the nuts. Botanist Peter Del Tredici, while on China's Tianmu Mountain conducting research for his doctoral thesis on ginkgos, saw red squirrels and palm civets carrying off the seeds. Leopard cats in China eat them, and in Japan, raccoon dogs and badgers find them alluring. Here in the United States, people have seen their dogs eat them (and, more frequently, roll in them). Eastern gray squirrels eat ginkgo nuts and I have seen a fox squirrel poking around a cluster of hanging ginkgo fruits.

That squirrel may have already eaten some of the seeds, but I didn't see it pluck any of them. Instead, it walked out along a spindly branch that rested on the bough of a neighboring pine— at least until the squirrel weighed it down and it gave way, sending the rodent tumbling. Just as quickly, the squirrel caught a branch with a rear paw and swung like that for a moment, not showing the slightest hint of alarm.

If the squirrel wasn't going to claim the fruit, I decided, I would. I picked one of the seeds and took it home.

The fruit was still green. The skin was frosted with white powder, like a Turkish delight. Beneath this was plump flesh, delicately mottled. The stem connected in a lopsided lump, like haphazardly melted wax. It didn't smell at all. I left it on my desk.

The Chemistry of Stench

One morning when I was nursing a cup of coffee at my desk, attempting to catch up with the Internet, I noticed that I was grinding my teeth. *Wait*, I thought, and I sniffed.

After a week, the ginkgo fruit had turned yellow, and started to collapse inward. I leaned close and inhaled, then jerked spasmodically backward. The smell was unmistakable. And though I'd thought it couldn't possibly be as bad as I had remembered, it was just as pungent. You know that moment in a horror movie when the protagonist opens a box and finds her best friend's corpse, along with the worms that have been eating him? The seed was the friend. I was the protagonist.

Surely this perfume is made up of many subtle parts, but the main olfactory chemical released by the seeds is butyric acid, which is also present in rancid butter and vomit. There is also hexanoic acid, which has a fatty, waxy, barnyard kind of smell. But the combination of these two acids' smells is not enough to describe the ginkgo fruit's stench. It's both of those things, plus a spritz of essential oils concentrated from a stout case of trench foot. An eighteenth-century Swedish naturalist, Carl Peter Thunberg, claimed that the Japanese ate the fleshy seed coat. I do not believe it.

I really had to get up close to smell it. This little fruit wasn't stinking up my whole office, it was just squeezing out the occasional jet of volatile chemicals. By the time these chemicals reached my nose, about two feet away, they were diffuse enough to affect my liminal perception without triggering a conscious response—at least for a little bit. I picked it up gingerly and carried it outside.

COOKING GINKGO

When people do eat ginkgo seeds, they remove the stinking flesh and roast the interior nuts. After a few more weeks, I resolved to try this. The juices in the fruits contain chemicals closely related to those in poison oak and ivy, so I put on blue latex gloves. Josephine also wanted to wear gloves, though they were far too big and fell off whenever she let her hands drop below her waist. When a food is forbidden to or declared inappropriate for her, like coffee, she insists that she loves it. But her reaction to the ginkgo seed was visceral: She wrinkled her nose, squinched her eyes, and pulled away with undeniable disgust.

In traditional production, I'd learned, people often bury the nuts until the fruit has rotted away and then dig them up again. A faster method involves immersing the seeds in water (to suppress the smell) and squeezing off the flesh by hand. I took a small bowl of water to the backyard and dropped my ginkgo seed inside. Josephine squatted beside me, intent. Most of the flesh came off with the first squeeze, and the rest was easy to rub away. The seed was a smooth tan oval, flaring to form a sharp edge along its longer circumference. I dumped the water on our flowerbed, tossed the flesh on the compost pile, and took the seed inside for one more wash under the faucet. It still smelled terrible. Josephine turned it over and over, then held it to her chest and did a little dance.

I poured cooking oil into a cast-iron pan and Josephine plopped in the seed. We cooked it over a high flame until the oil started to smoke and the seed turned brown, then I flipped it over, turned the burner down low, and covered the pan.

I'd read that it's important to cook the seeds to denature their toxins. Ginkgotoxin is similar in structure to vitamin B_6, and eating too much of it interferes with our ability to synthesize the vitamin. That can provoke a biochemical cascade that, especially in children, may lead to seizures, and even death. This sounds alarming, but it wasn't enough to deter me. Before I started researching plant chemistry, I divided the world of potential foods into two categories: things that are poisonous and things that aren't. But in reality everything is a little bit poisonous. It's the dose that matters, not the poison. All plants defend themselves with toxins, but usually at such low levels that they are harmless, and might even be good for us. There is a hypothesis that our immune system has evolved to rely on a continual barrage of plant chemicals to fine-tune its production of antioxidants. In other words, the very thing that makes vegetables healthy may be the fact that they are trying to kill us.

Ginkgo seeds, however, seemed more dangerous than, say, broccoli. But cooking is an effective way of breaking down the chemicals that plants construct (this can be a good or a bad thing, depending). To err on the side of caution, I let the seed cook in the pan for about fifteen minutes after turning down the flame. My hands were haunted by phantom itches while we waited. The power of suggestion was playing tricks on me, and though I'd been careful, some paranoid corner of my mind was convinced my fingers were about to break out into an itchy rash. Then, without thinking, I would rub my eyes and become intently aware of a prickling sensation around my eyelids.

When I finally took out the ginkgo seed, it was blackened on both sides, and I could feel the nut rattling around inside the thin shell. It shattered under a little pressure from a nutcracker. Something small, brown, and misshapen fell onto the table and immediately broke into several pieces. It looked like something that had melted and then solidified, and perhaps it had. Josephine snatched a flake.

"It's yummy!" she exclaimed.

I did not share her enthusiasm. The shard I crunched between my teeth was hard and tasteless, more like a shell than a nut. I picked up a mild burned odor and nothing else.

Beth's palate is several times more sensitive than mine, and she gingerly took the piece that Josephine offered and turned it over in her mouth.

"Oh yeah, it is pleasant," she allowed. "There is a sort of nuttiness."

Most of my piece had gotten stuck to my molars, and as it softened it became sweet and emitted a mild, toasty, butterscotch-like flavor. I must have cooked it so long that I'd not only denatured the toxins, but also caramelized the sugars in the seed. I'd have to try again, maybe with some instruction this time. Josephine took another small piece. "Mmm," she said with drama. "I *super* love it."

In his book on the ginkgo, Peter Crane includes a list of the flavor descriptions he came across:

"With a plump, soft, partly creamy, partly waxy white 'meat' not much bigger than a peanut, the ginkgo nut has a taste that has been variously described as like 'mild Swiss cheese,' 'pine nuts,' 'potatoes crossed with sweet chestnuts,' 'green pea crossed with Limburger cheese,' or just 'fishy.'" Ginkgo nuts are sold in Chinatowns around the world as *bai guo,* often inauspiciously translated as "semen ginkgo."

Yum? Crane writes that he has encountered ginkgo nuts most often baked in their shells on a tray, or in tinfoil. But they show up in both sweet and savory dishes—soups, stir-fries, desserts—in many different Asian culinary settings. In Japan the tradition of eating ginkgo nuts with sake goes back to at least 1758, when it was mentioned in the *Kaiseki-ryori-cho,* a book on traditional foods.

In the West you are more likely to hear about ginkgo as a medicine than as a food. In the popular imagination, it improves memory, prevents Alzheimer's disease, and cures erectile dysfunction. But there's good evidence only that it keeps blood vessels from constricting, perhaps aiding people who have insufficient blood flow in the brain. That is a common cause of dementia, so some doctors have suggested giving it to certain elderly patients.

Ginkgo supplement pills are derived from the green leaves from trees on plantations. The owners of these plantations keep the trees stubby to ease harvesting. Supplement makers claim that ginkgo has been used in Chinese medicine for thousands of years. That's true, but Chinese medicine employed the ginkgo nut, not the leaves. They used the seeds to prevent—among other things—drunkenness and hangovers. There's little evidence it works. Doctors are still wary of ginkgo because the chemical dose in each pill varies widely from one extract to the next, with no standardization and little regulation.

Ginkgo Cooked Right

After I overcooked my ginkgo seed I was determined to find someone who could show me how they were supposed to taste. Josephine and I returned to the trees and filled a bag with seeds, which by this time were spotting the sidewalk. I cleaned them and then took them to Carolyn Phillips's house, near San Jose. Phillips, a friend of a friend, had lived in Taiwan for eight years in the 1970s, and returned to the United States with a passion for Chinese food.

Phillips met me at the door, offered me slippers to replace my shoes, and ushered me into a house filled with Eastern art. She had short blond hair and a gaze so avidly focused that I found myself unconsciously matching her intensity, breathlessly peppering her with questions, even before we had perched on the couch.

Her husband, J. H. Huang, was as gentle as she was acute.

He ghosted in, accepted introductions with a smile, expressed regret that I hadn't been able to bring Josephine, then nodded to excuse himself and returned to his study, where he was reading Lao Tzu.

I'd wanted to find someone who understood the culinary tradition behind the cooking of ginkgo nuts because all the recipes I'd found in English were written by Westerners experimenting rather than drawing on East Asian history and practice. Phillips was well positioned to serve as a translator of culinary tradition: When she arrived in Taipei she found herself in the nexus of Chinese food cultures. When the Communists took over mainland China, many of the wealthy nationalists moved to Taiwan, she told me, and they brought with them cooks representing every regional tradition. "You have all the foods of China in one spot, all the most amazing foods. There were these incredible dining palaces. I just fell face-first into the cuisine." She became a student of Chinese foods and recently poured everything she had learned into a cookbook: *All Under Heaven: Recipes from the 35 Cuisines of China.*

As it turned out, there wasn't much to cooking ginkgo, but Phillips had also prepared a small feast so I could try the seeds in the proper context. She had used store-bought, precleaned seeds, but when I produced mine she rolled them in a hot wok, toasting them like popcorn. The meat that emerged when we cracked them was bright green—like jade, she said—utterly different from the shriveled brown product of my overcooking. The seeds were, to my surprise, nearly tasteless, and a bit tacky. It was like eating stiff gnocchi. After all I'd read about the flavor

of ginkgo, I'd expected them to be exciting and difficult, but
they were mild and starchy, with just the faintest hint of bitterness. They were bitter in the way some beers are, pricking the
taste buds just enough to make me take notice.
It's not all about flavor, Phillips told me. Chinese culinary
theory seeks to balance taste, texture, and color. For instance,
Phillips had made a stir-fry that emphasized textures, with
water chestnuts (very crunchy), cooked celery (somewhat
crunchy), ginkgo (gummy), and red goji berries (soft). The flavor
was delicious, but the contrasting textures, now that I knew to
pay attention to them, were even more interesting. She had also
made ginkgo braised with Napa cabbage, which brought out a
bit of bitterness in the seeds.

Ginkgo shows up all over China, Phillips said, though it's
not a common ingredient. The seeds are valued for their putative
medicinal properties, which is an underlying theme in Chinese
culinary theory. The cooks think about the health qualities traditional Chinese medicine ascribes to each ingredient.

Huang joined us for lunch, and the pair told stories from
Taiwan and from the hidden subcultures of Oakland's and San
Francisco's Chinatowns. I gorged on the ginkgo dishes, along
with soba noodles and smoked chicken. Partway through the
meal I realized I'd easily eaten at least ten seeds, and asked if
they thought I was in any danger. Phillips blinked. "I have *never*
heard that they could cause poisoning," she said. I wasn't too
concerned, because I had asked another cook, a woman born in
China, about toxicity and she laughed. "Americans always say
it's poison," she said. "No. This is American superstition." On

my own, I'd been hypervigilant, but there, eating good food
with thousands of years of tradition behind it, I felt no
concern.

ARBOREAL CHARISMA

What is it that makes ginkgos compelling? Peter Crane wrote:
"Ginkgo owes its resurgence in historical times not just to its
utilitarian value but also to some kind of irresistible biological
charisma that has taken hold in both Eastern and Western cultures." But what is this "irresistible biological charisma"?
Ginkgo is not one of those superlative organisms, like the giant
sequoia, or the blue whale, that is breathtaking because it's
shockingly out of scale with everything else we encounter. It
doesn't have brilliant colors or exhibit particularly startling
behavior, although ginkgo sex is strangely wonderful. And yet
people do form special relationships with these trees.

It must have something to do with their uniqueness. Ginkgos are different from the other species in this book in that
they are strange enough that they sometimes draw attention to
themselves. And once your eyes are tuned to see ginkgos, they
pop out at you. After noticing those smelly trees, I began to
see others: My nearest BART station is decorated with ginkgos, and there are several leggy youngsters within a block of
my house. The writer Nancy Ross Hugo says that immature
ginkgos are like "adolescent boys who don't know where to
put their fast-growing arms and legs." It's true: During the
period when the trunk is about the circumference of an arm,
ginkgos are in a hurry to grow all at once. "The widely spaced
branches create a scaffolding that looks more like a coatrack

than a tree," Hugo wrote. But then, perhaps around the age of thirty or so, when the trunk's circumference is closer to that of a thigh, leaves fill in this scaffold. While other trees turn many colors in the autumn, ginkgo leaves morph from green to gold. They begin to turn in late summer, and by about mid-November—depending on the latitude and the whims of the particular tree—they have transformed entirely. The trees are brilliantly uniform, each one a thick daub of yellow against the sky.

Perhaps it's this autumn beauty that inclines people toward ginkgos. When they grow older still, they become giants of great gravitas. In comparison to those massive craggy branches, the leaves are dots. You can see through their pointillist drapery to the interior architecture. They live for many hundreds of years. Careful reviews of historical records puts the oldest trees at about a thousand years, though some claim they are as much as four thousand years old. These big ginkgos—there are more than one hundred of them—are especially magnificent in the autumn.

Then the leaves fall: One day the golden leaves are aloft, and the next they are spread in a circle around the trunk. The fall is so dramatic that for many years the townspeople of Monroe, Wisconsin, held a competition to see who could most accurately guess the date the old tree outside the library would shed its leaves. "Ginkgo has the most synchronized leaf drop of any tree I know," Crane writes. I waited eagerly to note the day of my local leaf drop, but in the mild climate of coastal California it didn't happen quite as suddenly as the experts had described. Perhaps some ginkgos lost leaves faster than other trees, but not dramatically so. Who could blame them? The seasons here pass quietly, like a pulse beneath the skin.

None of the ginkgo's aesthetic qualities are all that different from those of other trees. I could just as easily wax poetic about the beauty of beech trees, or the majesty of ancient sugar pines. But I think that ginkgos are just unusual enough for the occasional human to take notice of them. It's not that any particular tree or breed of dog or varietal of rose is objectively superior to its peers, they just happen to be the creatures that momentarily capture our flickering attention. As soon as humans take open-hearted notice of anything in the natural world, we find reason to love it.

I came across one of those gawky juvenile trees on a sunny September afternoon. It was planted next to the same driveway where Josephine and I had pilfered acorns. It was small, shorter than I, and its leaves were turning yellow at their edges.

"Are you looking at that ginkgo tree?" someone called.

I looked for the speaker. Two women, one with white hair and one gray, were standing at the top of a slate-tiled stoop. They came down the steps.

"Isn't it wonderful?" said the white-haired woman. "It wants to grow every which way but up, though." She pointed to the top of the tree, which had broken off and was a lifeless stick. It had vigorous branches sprouting laterally.

I asked if she knew its sex.

"Well, it's funny you should ask. A friend of mine said, 'No matter what, don't get a male, because they smell awful.' But then I learned it's the females that smell, we had it backwards."

Nonetheless, this tree had never borne fruit, she said, so perhaps it was male after all. I explained that she wouldn't know for a long time, because ginkgos take twenty or thirty years to become sexually mature.

"Ah well," she smiled. "By then I would be a very old lady." As we parted, she told me to let her know if I learned anything about how to guide her ginkgo's growth upward rather than outward.

A few days later, I left a note for my neighbor on her stoop. I'd learned that ginkgos have two types of branches: fast-growing long shoots, and slow-and-steady short shoots, which produce leaves. Young ginkgos are almost entirely long shoots, which is why juveniles often look so leggy. If the uppermost long shoot dies, the nearest short shoots will transform to take over the job. This is true for all trees: When one loses the uppermost leader, a chemical signal will cue other branches to grow upward. Because ginkgos grow quickly and can sprout branches from any leaf shoot, they can be especially unruly. A gardener can restrain these upstarts by simply pruning off their tips, or by tying them to train the branches upward. An espaliered ginkgo covers a wall of the University of Cambridge plant sciences building like ivy: it is living proof they can be trained. But this is unusual and evidently takes a lot of work.

Tree Watching

Paying attention to the minutiae of how a tree grows sounds like the most boring possible occupation. Watch paint dry, and at least it's over in a few hours. Trees can grow for centuries.

But Nancy Ross Hugo and Robert Llewellyn, the creators of the remarkable book *Seeing Trees,* found that they actually couldn't keep up with the trees in their backyards. If you look at the big picture—the tree as it's growing—nothing happens. If, however, you notice the details—the leaves emerging, the flowers forming, the fruits bursting from the flowers—then trees seethe with action.

To capture this combination of large and small, Llewellyn used software to merge multiple photographs. The resulting images allow you to see these tree parts more clearly than you can in real life. Both the large and the small perspectives remain in focus, producing startling images. What looks like a radiant deep-sea creature turns out to be the vermillion pollen-releasing structure of a common red maple.

Trees will reward the observant. Watch closely in springtime and you can see how buds push outward from the wood and unfold their leaves. You can find the pollen distributors and pollen-receiving flowers. You can watch the seeds grow and transform, and finally watch the leaves fall. Hugo says that if you are willing to notice trees, you're likely to start thinking of fall as "a verb, not a noun. The action of leaves in air." The same is surely true of spring: It's not just a section of the calendar to be traversed, it's the springing forth of delicate, fleshy leaves from inanimate wood.

You don't have to climb to see this stuff. When a tree is too tall to see up into its branches, Hugo recommends looking down to see what has fallen. She tries not to call this material "litter." "I consider it detritus laden with treasures, like shells on a seashore."

A lot of these tree treasures are bizarre. Once you see one, you may wonder how you ever missed it. But you have to truly see it: Let it in, allow it to provoke your curiosity. We have a pair of magnolias in front of our house, and one day Josephine picked up a sort of cone from under these trees and asked me what it was. I said I didn't know. I'd seen these things so often that I could ignore them without ever wondering what they were up to.

But when I looked at a magnolia cone closely, I couldn't help but wonder. It looks like a Dr. Seuss character, with a fuzzy oblong head covered with stiff brown curls and a depilated neck. This cone, or follicetum, develops at the center of those big magnolia flowers. If it stays on the tree, it will grow much larger and produce red seeds. But sometimes, a squirrel or a crow dislodges a cone—or perhaps the tree aborts it—while it's still in this half-developed state.

When you decide to learn about one species, you inevitably learn about others, and I'd been seeing references to magnolias in ginkgo books. Magnolias are not an evolutionary loner like ginkgos—most of its family survived—but it has been around almost as long. Both kinds of trees grew a hundred million years ago, and both likely fed dinosaurs.

Tree of Time

Does it matter if something is a living fossil? The ginkgo is no more special than a relatively recent arrival like an oak, but it can open the doors of human perception a crack and provide a glimpse of eternity.

When the physician and writer Oliver Sacks was a boy, he had

a book called *Ancient Plants* by the paleobotanist Marie Stopes.
In Sack's *Island of the Colorblind*, he wrote that Stopes' book

> excited me strangely. . . . I got my first glimpse of deep
> time, of the millions of years, the hundreds of mil-
> lions, which separated the most ancient plants and
> our own. "The human mind," Stopes wrote, "cannot
> comprehend the significance of vast numbers, of
> immense space, or of aeons of time"; but her book,
> illustrating the enormous range of plants which had
> once lived on the earth—the vast majority long
> extinct—gave me my first intimation of such eons. I
> would gaze at the book for hours, skipping over the
> flowering plants and going straight to the earliest
> ones—ginkgos, cycads, ferns, lycopods, horsetails.

There is something eerie and wonderful in these plants that
have traversed the vastness of time, that have made their way
from an alien world of the past into our own world. When
Johannes Kepler confirmed the Copernican theory that Earth
was not at the center of the universe, he confessed to feeling a
"hidden and secret horror" at being lost in some obscure quad-
rant of the vastness. There's an old ginkgo on the UC Berkeley
campus that I visit sometimes, and when I lay my hands on its
rough bark and try to imagine its journey across time and space,
I can't quite replicate Kepler's horror, but sometimes, I do feel a
twinge of vertigo to be standing so close to the edge of deep time.
The probability—the number of coin flips for survival versus
extinction—that led to me and this tree breathing the same air is
mind-bogglingly low. It gives me an odd sense of camaraderie

with the tree. It's a raw, unsophisticated feeling, just: *Will you look at us, alive! Together!*

Sacks wrote lovingly about ginkgos, but he expressed this sense of camaraderie most clearly when writing about another living fossil, the cycad. Years after Sacks obsessed over *Ancient Plants,* he visited the cycads of Guam. He was surprised to find that a giant pollen cone of a cycad was warm to the touch; they generate heat, perhaps to spread insect-beckoning scents. Sacks, overcome by the "almost-animal warmth," impulsively hugged it "and almost vanished in a huge cloud of pollen."

I started this chapter by asking why people are inspired to plant *Ginkgo biloba,* but I suppose I was really asking, "What makes this tree special?" I've just filled pages with legitimate answers to that question. But at the same time, there's nothing special about ginkgo. Every tree could provide just as many wonders if we dedicated the same amount of time to its study and appreciation.

As I learned about ginkgos, I also picked up facts about the other trees in my neighborhood. I learned that the often-hated tree of heaven has bark that smells of peanut butter when scratched. The magnolias in front of my house, of course, became fascinating when I thought of them as triceratops fodder. I noticed the horse chestnuts lining a nearby street when I saw the squirrels harvesting their nuts, and I learned that these nuts, or "conkers," aren't good for eating, but children around the world attach them to strings and see whose can last longest when they bash them against each other. Oh, and there was the pinecone I dissected with Josephine, which revealed a single seed. When she asked why it was attached to its gauzy wing, I threw it up into the air so she could see it helicopter down, but then watched as an eddy in the wind caught the propeller and whirled it up into the sky and out of sight. I learned that almost all city trees are floodplain species, with roots that can survive submerged, by water or concrete.

We plant trees, and then forget to notice them. They are ornaments, and they are also infrastructure, cleaning the air, absorbing storm water, and cooling the sidewalks. They can also provide food. I, for one, am happy to have a couple female ginkgos nearby. Perhaps I'll begin gathering the seeds as an autumn tradition. But if nothing else, the stench forced me to pay attention, as I had as a child, to the meaning hidden in trees.

TURKEY VULTURE

JOSEPHINE, BREATHLESS AND WILD-EYED, found me in the kitchen. "Papa! There's an eagle!"

"Do you mean a seagull?"

"No, an *e*-gull!" She pointed outside.

I wiped my hands and followed her to the door. We got there just in time to see a black bird taking off from a tree, powering into the air on wings that might have been longer than my arms. Maybe it was an eagle—a golden eagle, perhaps? Then I saw the scrawny red head. It was a turkey vulture.

I'm generally disappointed when I see turkey vultures. Whenever I see something vaguely raptorlike gliding across the sky, I'll stop to see if I can identify a hawk or falcon—respectable birds worthy of note. But then I'll see the fingerlike feathers spread wide at the wingtips or the white on the underside of the wings and think, *Oh,* just *a turkey vulture.*

But after a year of researching wildlife so ubiquitous they are invisible, I couldn't turn away, or tell Josephine that her enthusiasm was misplaced. So what do we know about turkey vultures?

The answer: Not much. Turkey vultures have deflected the attention of scientists just as effectively as they had deflected mine. They are the introverts of the avian world, silently doing important work while more entertaining birds get all the love. This only made them more interesting to me: The more invisible a creature is, the greater its potential to enrich my life. Douglas Long, a biologist and longtime turkey vulture enthusiast, is going to write the first book on these birds as soon as he can get to it. When I asked around, several people told me that Long was the person to talk to about turkey vultures, and I began pestering him with e-mails. Eventually, we got in touch. He told me there are huge gaps in our understanding of turkey vultures. And that's odd, because they are so big, so readily visible in the sky.

"I think turkey vultures are probably the biggest least-studied birds in North America," Long told me. "What we know about golden eagles or bald eagles could fill books. No one has written a book on turkey vultures. Not that much is known about them."

"We have no real idea of what the current population is and what it was historically," he told me. We don't know how long they live, though there's a forty-year-old bird in captivity. "It's not like you cut off the wing and count the rings." Though we see the birds all around North and South America, scientists don't have a handle on their distribution or movements. These very basic facts about this very common bird are simply unknown. Turkey vultures are like an unassuming neighbor that you frequently see, but if you start asking around, you realize no one has ever talked to the guy. And all of a sudden, what had seemed too banal to notice becomes mysterious.

I mistake turkey vultures for hawks or falcons because all these birds are gliding strategists. All raptors are excellent gliders, but turkey vultures have mastered the art. They set their wings open and make only the subtlest muscular adjustments to maneuver. In this way they are able to hang on the breeze, expending minimal energy. They circle, buoyant in thin air, searching for food. An adult turkey vulture may take to the air in the morning and, after some gawky flapping to hoist itself skyward, spend the next twelve hours aloft, motionless as it traverses vast expanses. Turkey vultures spend 90 percent of the daylight hours soaring, Long said. They ride rising bubbles of warm air called thermals up to 5,000 feet, then spiral slowly down. They can go higher—up to 20,000 feet. We only know they reach that altitude because they have hit airplanes far above where pilots expect to see birds.

A HYGIENE PROBLEM

Long had agreed to meet me at a brewery. He told me to look for "the chubby middle-aged guy in a Hawaiian shirt." I wouldn't call him chubby: He has a Falstaffian solidity, and the jovial bonhomie to match. Long's interest in wildlife biology stems from a childhood filled with animals, he told me. As a baby, he slept alongside cats in his crib, and there were many more creatures in the backyard of his Orange County, California, home. "In the place where neighbors would have swimming pool or a tennis court, we had a walk-through aviary filled with birds and a koi pond."

This interest in animals eventually took him to the California Academy of Sciences, where he did research on sharks, birds, and manatees. He also established a turkey vulture colony on the roof of the museum and began delving in to the mysteries of these strange birds.

Long and I found a table on the roof deck of the brewery. I bought him craft beer and peppered him with questions. To start off, I wanted to know why turkey vultures stay up in the air for all those hours on end.

"Well, right, that's one question," he said. "Presumably they spend all that time in the air because it's hard to find food; they have to move around a lot to locate dead animals. But that raises all sorts of other questions." How do they eat carcasses without getting sick? How does their extreme mobility affect their lives? Do they return to regular homes? And how do they manage this life suspended in midair when they have to molt and replace their feathers? One of the most stubbornly bewildering mysteries about turkey vultures, he said, has to do with their strange proclivity for pooping on their legs. Several common theories attempt to explain this, but none stands up to scrutiny. "You'll see these 'fun facts' about turkey vultures on the Web," Long said, "and they'll often say turkey vultures defecate on their legs to cool off. Well, in this colony we had in San Francisco, they were doing that in the coldest part of winter." So that doesn't make any sense. This awkward mystery concerning a sometimes-awkward bird, I figured, was a good place to start.

Intestinal Fortitude

Here's a slightly better explanation for the leg pooping: It armors the vultures by covering their feet with good germs that fight off the pathogens swarming in their food. This is plausible: Turkey vultures are always coming into contact with virulent microbes, and they have other, similarly bizarre means of protecting themselves.

It's not that turkey vultures like rotten meat, Long said. When he gave the birds in his colony a choice, their preferences were always clear. "We did simple experiments," he said. "Here's meat from a dead sea lion that's been on the beach for a week, and here's fresh meat that we just got in Chinatown. They went for the fresh stuff, always."

But they generally eat rotten meat, because that's what they can find. Turkey vultures use their noses to detect the chemicals produced by decomposition, then zero in on the source. This capability is unusual—most birds have a weak sense of smell, or none at all. You sometimes hear that you aren't supposed to touch a baby bird because the mother will reject it if it smells wrong: "It's a myth," Long said. "The mother would never notice the difference." Turkey vultures, on the other hand, are equipped with olfactory organs that can pick out a few molecules of decay, even diluted in the wash of high-altitude wind. When a turkey vulture detects the scent of rot, it circles down, tracing the plume of chemicals to its source. They are so good at zeroing in on dead things that other animals use them as guides. California condors, for instance, don't have such a great sense of smell, so they follow turkey vultures and then bully the smaller birds away from the prize. Humans also watch turkey vultures:

In Florida, a Dade County Sheriff's officer told Long that he will always check when he sees the birds circling, because you never know—it could just be a dead alligator, or it could be a human body.

Once a turkey vulture finally lands beside its festering quarry, it faces a more formidable challenge: It has to actually eat the thing. Sometimes it's a healthy animal that a car dispatched, but other times it's an animal that died from disease. The vultures have no way of differentiating between diseased and healthy as they gulp down the raw meat and organs. But turkey vultures have incredibly powerful stomach acids that seem to wipe out anything they touch. "This has been the subject of a lot of curiosity, but very little medical research," Long told me. "They will eat something with a very high *E. coli* or *Listeria* load and they will be fine. They can eat stuff that's tested positive for rabies, *Hantavirus,* cholera; when it comes out the other end, there's just no trace. They are virtually indestructible."

In the 1930s, after an outbreak of hog cholera in livestock, the USDA worried that turkey vultures were spreading germs and advised farmers to shoot them. As we now know, the birds were actually doing the opposite: disinfecting tainted meat in the crucibles of their stomachs.

Still, Long doesn't exactly buy the idea that turkey vultures poop on their legs as an extension of this microbial warfare. The problem, he said, is that the bird's legs don't have a lot of contact with the carcasses. Their faces, on the other hand, are covered with germs. The vultures have a hard time breaking through tough animal hides, so they frequently find one opening—yes, sometimes it's the anus—where they insert their heads. One study found 528 different types of microorganisms on turkey vultures' faces (compared to just 76 in their guts). "Maybe their poop kills germs, but most of the germ contact is on the face," he said. "So if that's the explanation, they should be pooping on their faces."

They don't do that. Another theory bites the dust.

Vulture Vomit

A turkey vulture has barfed on Long, providing him with a first-hand experience of the stomach detoxification process.

"It smells absolutely abhorrent," he said. "It's hard to wash off your hands. It's one of those smells you wash three or four times and it's still there."

"And it smells like rotten meat?" I guessed.

"It's rotten meat, plus. Maybe it's that super enzyme they have in their stomachs, or maybe it's some sort of beneficial bacterial. It's penetrating, and super distinctive—a special turkey vulture smell."

It was one turkey vulture in particular that would puke on Long. One of the birds in his colony had imprinted on humans when it was young, and it acted more like a puppy than a vulture. It would affectionately lean on you, Long said, and begged to be scratched on the neck. Turkey vultures in the wild are almost asocial: They roost in groups, but they don't interact with, talk with, or preen each other. But they are also very clever, and this particular bird had simply learned how to emote in a way that humans could understand.

In any case, Long would take this bird to demonstrations and school lectures. He'd simply put it in the back seat of the car, which always worked fine unless he had to drive a particularly windy road. Then it would get carsick and vomit, and the whole car would stink for weeks.

Turkey vultures seem to use their vomit as a form of defense. If threatened by a larger animal, they will extend their wings and hiss. If this doesn't work, they vomit up their last meal. This may startle the aggressor, or it may simply lighten their load so they can take to the air more easily. It might also be an offering: *Eat this, not me.* Long has seen coyotes surprise turkey vultures with what appears to be intention and then gobble up the smelly regurgitated mess. Isn't nature beautiful?

Unorthodox Perfume

Why, then, do turkey vultures poop on their legs? The short answer is that no one knows. It's another secret hiding in plain sight. Long does have a hunch; he calls it a "crazy idea" to make it perfectly clear that he hasn't tested it in any scientific way. But he has spent enough time watching turkey vultures to have a sense of how they work and suspect it may have something to do with signalling identity.

The birds he kept on the roof of the California Academy of Sciences all looked very similar, but he said "it was easy to tell which was which from their personalities." There was Friendly the affectionate bird, Tennessee Jack the delinquent teenager that loved running behind houses at night and stealing dog food until someone caught it with a pool net, Lumpy, Droopy, and Maggie, who was alert and ornery. The five of them were all intelligent, curious, and incredibly destructive when bored.

("They figured out how to dig up the wood chips, and then found the corner of the tarp under that, and then they peeled the tar paper off the roof," Long remembered. "So I would have to do things like bury dead rats under layers of cardboard to keep them occupied.") And he noticed that whenever the birds encountered each other, each would lower their heads to the level of the other's legs. Were they sniffing?

Though Long could easily recognize the birds by name, they didn't know if they were male or female. There's simply no way to tell the sex from the outside, Long said. Then, for an experiment that required that information, Long had a veterinarian make a small incision to find out what kind of sex organs each bird had. Long and the other researchers had, out of force of habit, started calling some birds "him," and others "her," but when the results came in they found that they'd assumed the wrong sex for every bird except one.

If the researchers had such a hard time sexing the birds, how did the turkey vultures themselves do it? Perhaps—and Long reminded me that this was "just a crazy idea"—they were smelling each other's legs to determine who was a male and who was a female. Maybe there is some revealingly fragrant hormone in turkey vulture feces, which they deliberately apply to their legs.

This doesn't seem so crazy. Any woman who has ever walked into a heavily used men's room can tell you that male urine smells different. Transgender people undergoing testosterone therapy to transition from female to male have noted the same thing. But Long's turkey vulture hypothesis will remain a crazy idea until someone has the time and money to figure it out. Like so many other basic facts about turkey vultures, it's a mystery tantalizingly close to resolution.

After a couple of beers, I'd exhausted Long's well of facts. "We need more science," he said with a shrug. And if anyone wants to study them, they are right outside. Just look up.

A not-so-secret part of me wants Josephine to grow up to be the sort of science whiz who might solve these *vitally* important mysteries, but turkey vulture–watching was pretty boring for her. I'd point one out and she would spot the bird, but after about a minute she'd ask, "When will it find a dead animal?"

Unless you are lucky enough to stumble upon a roost or a carcass, you aren't likely to see more from a turkey vulture than endless circling. I love seeing them do that; I like to imagine they are sweeping calligraphy across the sky. Nonetheless, I don't have enough patience to decode this script, and Josephine has even less. So I moved our bird-watching inside, where we found more exciting footage on the computer: A turkey vulture eating a fish, a raccoon, a flattened squirrel.

"Would you like some dead squirrel guts to eat?" I asked Josephine.

She twisted around in my lap and smiled at me. "Can we be a turkey vulture family?" she asked.

Sure, of course.

She slid to the floor and ran into the dining room, waving her arms. "Flap, flap, flap, glide!" she chanted. I followed her, doing my best impression of the terrifying turkey vulture hiss-scream.

Josephine pointed toward the window seat: "Look, Papa Turkey Vulture, a dead squirrel! And a dead hamster!"

We ate them all, leaving only the bones.

RESILIENT TRAVELERS

Once upon a time, around the last ice age, there were many more large mammals in the Americas. There were mammoths, mastodons, three species of bison, giant sloths, and giant camels. Back then, there was a lot more dead meat around, and there were many more kinds of vultures to eat it: There are several extinct teratorns, as researchers named them, including one species with an eighteen-foot wingspan, and another (in South America) that weighed up to 175 pounds. Those big mammals went extinct (humans, or an asteroid, or some combination may have killed them), and when those meat sources disappeared, the vultures died out too. There are just three species left in North America: California condors, which are barely hanging on; black vultures inhabiting the southeastern United States and Mexico; and turkey vultures, which have been the most adept survivors. You'll see them everywhere from Patagonia to Alaska. They had stayed away from the far north, but as climate change warms the world there are reports from Inuit people in northern Nunavut of "bald ravens," which have turned out to be a new (and apt) name for turkey vultures.

Those birds not only adapt well to change, they seem to thrive on it. When white people wiped out the buffalo, turkey vultures transitioned to feeding on dead farm animals and scraps from slaughterhouses. With the inventions of the automobile and the modern landfill, turkey vultures expertly flexed to exploit these new food sources.

Their strategy for survival is travel light. Though they look big, their body mass is low: They weigh only three to six pounds. They have hardly any fat reserves. When gliding during the day, they burn barely any energy. If they are low on calories they go into a state of torpor at night, their body temperature and metabolism plummeting, their heart rate and digestion slowing down. They aren't muscular and fast like hawks, and they don't have a cushion of fat to see them through hard times like ducks do. Instead, they've thrived for thousands of years by carrying as little baggage as possible. These introverts of the avian world, so lacking in social graces, have no use for excess or flamboyancy. And so we ignore them. Watch turkey vultures and they'll show you how the invisible currents of air cascade through the sky, and where some other unseen animal has recently met its end. But mostly, turkey vultures remain a symbol of mystery. When the world surrounding the pattern of work, sleep, and commute starts to feel desperately straightforward and lacking in mystery, just look up at the bird kiting a clean line through the sky and remind yourself: There goes one of the great enigmas of the natural world.

ANT

ONCE I BECAME A FATHER, I started noticing insects (or "itty bugs," as Josephine called them), because I was spending a lot more time close to the ground. Moving your face into close proximity with the earth is the key to knowing insects, says Brian Fisher, an ant specialist at the California Academy of Sciences. "You have to go outside, just get a quarter of an inch above the ground, and watch them," he said. "And you'll see a whole new world opening up. This small world of insects is actually what's holding our society together."

This isn't hyperbole. E. O. Wilson, the patriarch of ant science, has said that insects are so important that if all the land arthropods disappeared, humans wouldn't be able to survive for more than a few days. But we are mostly unaware of the ways in which insects support us, not to mention all the cool stuff they do.

No matter where you are right now, if you walk outside looking for wildlife, the first animal you'll find is likely to be an insect, perhaps an ant. Ants are everywhere, in such abundance that we tune them out like we tune out traffic noise. Lean on a tree for a while and, whether you are in Cincinnati or Kamchatka, eventually you'll catch yourself brushing an ant off your hand. Get down on your haunches to examine any patch of lawn, or woods, or pavement, and sooner or later you'll find ants. Scientists doing back-of-the-napkin math have estimated that the total weight of ants is about equal to the total weight of humanity.

When I started trying to gain some familiarity and sense of neighborly understanding with my local ants, I hit a barrier that I hadn't encountered before: too much information. I could handle pigeons or ginkgos because that was only one species at a time. When I began looking at the handful of common squirrel species, I just had to be careful I wasn't mixing up a quirk of an eastern gray with that of a fox squirrel. But ants contain swarming multitudes. A researcher in 2003 tallied the number of ant species at 11,006. Five years later, another scientist updated the count to 12,467. We know a lot about just a few of these species, and almost nothing about the rest of them. Furthermore, scientists estimate that there are another ten thousand ant species waiting to be discovered. Anyone who wants to learn about these most common of insects faces a high hurdle: There are libraries full of information about ants, and yet that's barely the beginning of what there is to learn.

The vastness of the world of ants is an impediment for beginners, but it's also an enticement: It means that the unknown is waiting right there in the park and in the driveway, ripe for discovery. This quotidian exploration doesn't seem as exciting as trekking through jungles and seeking hidden empires, but people who have had the full range of these experiences say they are much more similar than you'd expect.

As a kid, scientist Rob Dunn dreamed of journeying into the

unknown, and as a biologist, he's actually gotten to do that. He has explored tropical forests and discovered things previously unknown to science. Having experienced all that, however, he reports that he now finds backyards even more fantastical. "New species, and even whole societies remain to be studied in the dirt beneath our feet," Dunn wrote. "Among the least explored empires are those of the ants."

WHAT KIND OF ANTS?

The first step, I figured, was to make out what type of ants I was dealing with. Scientists at North Carolina State University (NCSU)—where Dunn works—have set up a citizen-science project to identify ants around the United States (schoolofants. org). Its protocol is simple: Break cookies (pecan sandies; I'd learn why later) onto index cards, leave them outside for an hour, then dump all the ants that have accumulated on the cards into bags and send them off to NCSU for identification. I couldn't find index cards, so Josephine and I cut notebook paper into three-by-five-inch pieces. Using markers, we labeled four "green" and four "paved," then set out the bait. Josephine intently crumbled the cookies onto the cards. She had never had pecan sandies, and decided that they were strictly for ants. I did my best to preserve that illusion. It seemed like a winning strategy until Josephine told me she'd dumped the entire box of cookies outside, to facilitate our collection.

We waited exactly one hour, then went to check the bait. There was an acute absence of ants and the cookies were undisturbed, except for the mound of crumbs on one card: Those had disappeared entirely and the paper was standing on end across the yard. "Maybe the squirrel ate it," Josephine speculated. Then she confirmed, "Yes. It did."

This, it seemed to me, was an illustration in miniature of how we humans deal with mystery: We take the limited set of characters and causes we already know (ants, squirrels, cookies) and spin stories around them, until storytelling slips into certainty. We aren't overwhelmed by ants in my part of the world, but I was surprised that we didn't catch any. I began to spin my own theories. It had rained heavily the day before—the first real rain after a long drought—and I decided that perhaps the local colonies were too busy with flood repair to send out foragers. This is how we humans deal with mystery.

I would later learn that many ants deal with flooding fairly well. Lots of species can survive submerged for hours; some can even live underwater for days. Species that invest in expansive nests, like harvester ants, do spend time making flood repairs. But others can simply pick up and move when the waters rise.

Often it's not water, but the lack of it that threatens ants. Their eggs and larvae quickly dry up if the humidity is too low. And yet ants thrive in deserts around the world by gathering dew and extracting moisture from food. Some species balance water droplets on their mandibles and carry them down into their tunnels (the surface tension of a small drop is great enough that it remains intact when suspended across the mouthparts). *Diacamma rugosum* ants in India build rudimentary mist-harvesting devices by placing feathers around the entrance of their nests.

TO BE AN ANT

Ants are bizarrely unlike people, and yet there's a hint of human behavior at work in ant colonies. They are just strange enough, while also being similar enough, to prick the imagination. This has led thinkers throughout history to compare ants to people. Why aren't we more like them? Or are we actually more akin to ants than we'd like to believe?

When King Solomon suggested that people should be more like ants, he was making a point about industriousness and self-motivation:

> Go to the ant, thou sluggard; consider her ways, and be wise:
> Which *having no guide, overseer, or ruler,*
> Provideth her meat in the summer, and gathereth her food in the harvest. (my emphasis)

Ants are kind of amazing in this way if you think about it. They don't have bosses or leaders, or a corporate structure or hierarchy. They don't procrastinate. They don't need deadlines. There is no top-down organization.

And the normal bottom-up drivers of individual behavior— the itch to reproduce and the instinct for self-preservation— don't provide a tidy explanation for the motivations of ants either. The worker ants are all sterile females that can't reproduce, and self-preservation obviously isn't a priority, because they will sacrifice their lives to improve the fitness of the colony. A few workers of a Brazilian species, for instance, doom themselves to certain death each night by staying outside to seal up the entrance to the nest.

What makes an ant go? And what makes its actions contribute to the long-term strength of the colony, when it is neither controlled by a commander nor compelled by selfishness? It's all very well for Solomon to call me a sluggard and tell me to be more like an industrious ant, but how do I accomplish this when I don't even know how ants manage it? Corporate leaders and business theorists would love to figure this out. So would anarchists. Peter Kropotkin, the nineteenth-century anarchist philosopher, was fascinated by ants, and entranced by the possibility that humans might emulate them to achieve grand societal goals without leadership. In fact, the mysteries of ant behavior mirror two of the great questions of philosophy: How do we live together, and how do we attain a meaningful life?

Ant behavior starts to make a lot more sense if you think of the ants not as individuals, but as the cells of a body. It's a metaphorical body—a body politic if you like. But there's less friction in ant politics than in ours, because every ant in the colony has the same goal: Feed the queen and enable her to reproduce.

The queen is the ant that starts a colony. She lays the eggs that become all the other ants in the colony. Like an organism, the colony behaves as a unitary whole. It changes as it grows and has a clear life cycle. It has attributes of size, behavior, and complexity that are consistent throughout a species. The queen is its reproductive organ, and the workers are the digestive and circulatory systems.

Ants move resources around the colony by transferring food and water from mouth to mouth. Think of the colony's tunnels as veins and the ants as blood cells running through them. Each ant has a second stomach, which serves as an internal backpack. If an ant needs food, she'll tap a sister with an antenna, and the other ant will then provide her with a mouthful of pre-chewed snacks.

The queen sometimes lays eggs for food. They aren't living eggs—they don't grow into ants—but they are otherwise identical in composition. This egg cannibalism is simply a way to move nutrients around within the colony, just as a cell releases sugar into the bloodstream for use by hungrier cells. When the queen has plenty of nutrients and workers don't have enough, she can share her surplus by laying these eggs.

A queen can also do the opposite. If she's lacking in nutrients, she can suck the hemolymph—the ant "blood"—from developing larvae. She makes a small incision that heals quickly, and the young seem none the worse for it.

Thinking of a colony as a single organism can explain why workers do labor and sacrifice their lives without any possibility of individual reward. What these ants are striving for, from an evolutionary perspective, is to pass on their genes, but by proxy. They can't give birth, so they rely on the queen, who shares 50 percent of their genes. The only way for a worker ant to increase her reproductive fitness is to improve the fitness of the colony. It's wrong to suppose they are altruistic. Yes, they work tirelessly and martyr themselves without hesitation, but it's out of the selfish motivation to perpetuate their colony's genes.

The Wisdom of the Swarm

We have an inkling of what drives individual ants, but this opens a greater mystery: How do these individual actions add up to a colony acting with what looks like an informed strategy? Say I'm an ant going about my daily business, trying to help my colony succeed; what do I do? Should I go out and look for food? Cart larvae around? Dig new tunnels? Start moving the colony to a new location? Go to war? How can a part comprehend the needs of the whole?

Deborah Gordon has been watching harvester ants in Arizona for years, trying to figure this out. She and her students paint the ants with multicolored codes so they can track individuals to see what choices they make. Gordon has found that the ants pay attention to each other and switch tasks based on the chemical signals they pick up from their neighbors. If an ant is struggling to pull a big cricket back to the nest, the nearest ants may smell that struggle and go to help, perhaps releasing chemical "Workers Needed" signals of their own. "The pattern of interactions is the message," Gordon wrote. From the interplay and spread of individual actions emerges something that looks like intelligence.

The idea of emergent intelligence is wonderfully spooky. But we shouldn't glamorize it. This system is inefficient: Gordon found that large numbers of ants seem to do nothing all day. And if you've ever watched ants, you've seen them working at cross-purposes. That worker you recruited to help you pull that grasshopper may start pulling it in the opposite direction.

Of course, in human politics, people are *always* pulling in opposite directions. Could Kropotkin have been right? Instead of trying to agree on big societal strategies, which often fail anyway, would it work to simply pay close attention to our neighbors? It's enticing to think that we might be able to give up election campaigns, political theorists, Federal Reserve members, city planners, military generals, and environmental regulators and instead sense (and fulfill) the needs of society through interactions with our neighbors. This, I suspect, would be an unmitigated disaster, but that doesn't stop me from envying ants.

Imagine if you lived without conscious strategy or struggle in the assurance that your actions made a meaningful contribution to the commonwealth. What a gift it would be to simply know your place in the world, and to have no desire except to fill that role. Think of what it would be like to do away with all philosophizing and searching for meaning, all restlessness, all self-recrimination, all disappointment and anomie, and instead to simply do what you were meant to do.

And yet, I would object to being reincarnated as an ant. Though I'm constantly plagued by my second-guessing mind, I also find it's incredibly useful. It (usually) keeps me from being duped. Whereas ants trust and cooperate, humans search for ulterior motives. Self-doubt is a burden, but the task of doubting others, the work of skepticism, investigation, and critical analysis brings me great satisfaction. My doubting, self-sabotaging mind is a pain in the neck, but it's also, well, me.

Slavers and Parasites

The robotic quality of ant behavior—their ability to satisfy the needs of their colony without self-interest or apparent self-doubt—makes them perfect targets for con artists. Ants recognize their sisters by scent, but they don't seem to distinguish between individuals. So, with just the right perfume, various species—beetles, mites, wasps, millipedes, flies, and others—are able to slip into the colony undetected. There is a rove beetle that uses a series of chemical signals to convince ants that it is a foundling infant somehow misplaced from the nursery. The ants carry the beetle home to the brood chamber, groom it, and feed it when it begs for food. This attentive care isn't quite enough, however: The beetles also eat some of the ant larvae and eggs.

The rove beetle is just one of hundreds of species of ant parasites. As ant scientists E. O. Wilson and Burt Hölldobler put it in *Journey to the Ants*, "It is as though a human family were to invite gigantic lobsters, midget tortoises, and similar monsters to dinner, and never notice the difference."

Ants can also be parasites themselves. Amazon ants, *Polyergus breviceps*, which live all around the Northern Hemisphere, hack into the simple information-sharing systems of other ant colonies to enslave them. To start a colony, an Amazon queen finds a nest of *Formica* ants and battles her way to the royal chamber. Howard Topoff, at the Arizona Museum of Natural History, had watched these heists and described them in an article for *Scientific American*.

> In most cases the *Polyergus* queen quickly detects the entrance and erupts into a frenzy of ruthless activity. She bolts straight for the *Formica* queen, literally pushing aside any *Formica* workers that attempt to grab and bite her, . . . using her powerful mandibles for biting her attackers and a repellant pheromone from her Dufour's gland in her abdomen. With the workers' opposition liquidated, the *Polyergus* queen grabs the *Formica* queen and bites her head, thorax

and abdomen for an unrelenting twenty-five minutes. Between bouts of biting she uses her extruded tongue to lick the wounded parts of the dying victim. Within seconds of the host queen's death the nest undergoes a most remarkable transformation. The *Formica* workers behave as if sedated. They calmly approach the *Polyergus* queen and start grooming her—just as they did their own queen. The *Polyergus* queen, in turn, assembles the scattered *Formica* pupae into a neat pile and stands triumphally on top of it. At this point, the colony takeover is a done deal.

While the colony she has usurped feeds her, the *Polyergus* queen begins laying her own eggs. Eventually the *Polyergus* army rises up, supported by the *Formica* slaves. This army will, of course, eventually run out of slaves, because, without a queen, the stock of *Formica* workers will not be replenished. It is a crisis because *Polyergus* cannot survive without slaves. They cannot dig tunnels, or care for the young in the nursery. Amazon ants are slavers through and through, so dependent on this way of life that they no longer recognize food they pass on the ground: They only eat what slaves have chewed for them.

Weaponry and Diplomacy

Ants have an amazing armamentarium. Amazon ants make their raids using chemical propaganda signals, sending their victims dashing about aimlessly while they move in. A Malaysian *Camponotus* species can become a suicide bomber, blowing itself up and splattering all around it with green venom. *Pachycondyla tridentata* has a poisonous sting for big adversaries and the ability to produce sticky foam to bog down smaller attackers. Others are covered in spiked armor.

It's not all violence among ants. There are species that can work together, like carpenter and acrobat ants. These two share a nest and cooperatively maintain gardens high up in trees. There are beggar ants that subsist entirely on the rubbish from another species' nest. There are thief ants that live by stealing food from others. Even when ants have a direct confrontation, they generally try to avoid carnage. When two ants meet, they will touch antennae, reading the scent conveyed by the pattern of molecules on the other ant like a bar code. If it turns out that they are from different colonies, they try to avoid a fight through ritualized posturing: They open their mandibles as wide as possible, rear up on their back legs, and lift their abdomens threateningly. Often one ant will back down, averting violence.

Ant Language

Ants communicate primarily via scents. Every ant is coated in a layer of waxy hydrocarbons that volatilize, giving off the unique smell of the tribe. Ants also have a collection of glands spread throughout their bodies that contain ten to twenty chemicals. These are mixed in different proportions to convey different messages. E. O. Wilson and others dissecting ants under microscopes have been able to separate the chemical organs. Wilson found that when he wrote his name using the invisible fluid from one gland as ink, the ants followed the trail, making his signature visible with their bodies. When another of the chemicals was applied to an ant, her family became convinced that she was dead and deposited her in the trash heap; when she crawled away, they forcefully returned her to this cemetery.

Gordon says these experiments only give us the faintest understanding of chemical ant language. The meaning of each scent depends on its intensity, its combination with other chemicals, and the context: A smell that means one thing inside the nest might mean something very different in the middle of a battlefield. Exposing ants to chemical scents and trying to learn their meaning by watching the ants' reactions, she writes, is like an alien trying to learn English by blaring the word "ant" at New York City and watching the human response.

What do these chemical messages smell like? Some chemicals don't register in the scent receptors in our noses, or they exist in such tiny quantities that we can't pick them up. But ant scientists tell me that all these chemicals together give some species a signature smell. Most ants carry the vinegary scent of formic acid, and some species smell strongly of citronella. If you crush just the heads of ants in the genus *Odontomachus,* they smell like chocolate. Weaver ants smell and taste like limes (it's always worth tasting ants), and army ants smell like rotting meat or burnt hair. The chemical that gives odorous house ants their smell is nearly identical to the chemical that makes blue cheese stinky.

THE BACKYARD VELDT

Two weeks after our failed experiment as citizen-scientist ant collectors, we tried again. This time I was pickier about the locations. Instead of dropping the cards at random, I put them in spots where I'd seen ants before. There's a piece of pressure-treated wood separating the grass from a row of ferns and camellias running along our fence, and as I peered down at this

board I saw an ant walking purposefully forward. Another
came toward it from the opposite direction. When they met
they paused, tapped each other with their antennae, then continued on their way. I had found a trail. I set my index card
squarely across this line of movement, put a quarter of a cookie
atop it, and then sprinkled the crumbs stuck to my fingertips
all around it.

Half an hour later, Josephine and I went back to check our
bait. Not an ant in sight.

"Let's just watch this one on the board for a while," I told
Josephine. I sat down cross-legged on the grass, and she sank
into my lap. There were no ants to be seen, but as I scanned the
ground, other movements began to pop out at me. A brown
beetle about half the size of a three-year-old's pinky-nail clip-
ping dashed to the curving edge of a brown camellia leaf. It
wiggled its long, pennantlike tail.

I pointed. "What do you think that is, Josephine?"

"An orckrises," she said confidently.

For all I knew, she could have been right. There are some
four hundred thousand beetle species, many more than there are
of ants. (J. B. S. Haldane, one of the founders of evolutionary
biology, joked that if there were a creator that shaped each creature, he must have had an inordinate fondness for beetles.) Perhaps Josephine had just named a new species. Perched on the
leaf, it opened its shell, unfurled onionskin wings, and tumbled
gracelessly into the grass.

Another beetle, a shiny round fellow, like a ladybug of one-
tenth the normal size, trundled along nearby. A tiny, long-armed
white spider was performing calisthenics on a dried leaf. A fly of

some sort glided by noiselessly. A red spider mite dashed up a blade of grass and ran in circles on a leaf like an overcharged windup toy. A wolf spider of monstrous size compared to these itty bugs surprised us by taking a few steps out of a hiding place under the pressure-treated board. If I were being exhaustive, I could fill a book dedicated solely to the creatures we spied in a square foot of lawn.

Josephine called me back to the task at hand. An ant had ventured onto our index card. It lifted its head high, waving its antennae. Then it made a thorough investigation, touching the cookie from all sides and stopping to inspect the smaller crumbs. It did not pick anything up, and left the way it had come. I expected that this ant was going for reinforcements, but when other ants appeared, they came from another direction, following the trail I'd originally noticed. These ants bumped into crumbs and proceeded hastily around them. It was clear that these ants were not interested in pecan sandies. Perhaps they were some unusual sort of ant, I thought hopefully; perhaps I was about to identify a species that does not love sugar. I'd soon find out that I was wrong about the ants and the cookie's enticing qualities: They are both sugary *and* fatty. But this only deepened the mystery: What was this ant that crawled over delicious food without any sign of interest?

Josephine plucked a bud from the camellia bush and peeled back the petals. She'd been quietly absorbed for half an hour— longer than she usually sits still for just about anything, except cartoons. But eventually she got up and wandered off. My own mind meandered. Then I saw it: a dark cluster on a camellia bud. Aphids. And there, sure enough, were three ants standing guard, patrolling their little herd. Perhaps the ants were ignoring my cookies because they were intent upon the aphids. I leapt up and found Beth and Josephine in the living room. "I found what the ants are eating," I announced. "Come see."

The aphid-covered bulb was at about Josephine's eye level. "What's that—all that black stuff?" She wrinkled her nose. The aphids were so tightly packed they looked like a solid patch of fungus.

"Lots of little bugs," I said. "Do you see the ants climbing on top of them? They herd the aphids like cows and milk them."

"Milk them?" Beth said.

"Yeah, the aphids express a sugary liquid called honeydew from the anus."

"And the ants eat that when they could have pecan sandies?" Beth joked.

I reached into the camellia bush and plucked the twig supporting the blossom. At the first tremor, the guardian ants began running frantically around the cluster of leaves, waving their antennae. They were looking, I suppose, for whatever might have landed to attack their herd. I carried the twig inside and dropped it in an empty strawberry jelly jar.

Aphid Herding

Insect livestock are the most reliable source of sugar for many ants. Ants most frequently herd insects from the order Hemiptera, of which aphids are one example. They are herbivores that suck the juices from plants and excrete the excess sugars in the honeydew. Some aphids produce their body weight in honeydew

every hour, and if ants aren't harvesting it, the sugar can pile up
to such an extent that it makes it worthwhile for people to
gather it. According to Wilson and Hölldobler, "The manna
'given' to the Israelites in the Old Testament account was almost
certainly the excrement of the scale insect *Trabutina mannip-
ara,* which feeds on tamarisk. The Arabs still gather the material, which they call man." In Australia, honeydew is called
sugar lerp, and one person can collect three pounds of the stuff
in a day.

If you turn up your nose at eating excrement, you should
know that you may have already done it: A lot of honey comes
not from the nectar of flowers, but from this honeydew, which
bees collect from leaves. Essentially, this honey is insect poop
that's been processed inside another insect and then vomited up.

WHAT THE HELL AM I LOOKING AT?

There were two ants and several dozen aphids on the camellia
bud I'd dropped into my jelly-jar terrarium. One ant ventured
out to explore the jar while the other stayed behind. Then they
switched roles. I imagined that they were coordinating their
efforts so that their flock always had a guard.

I was eager to identify the ants, and optimistic that I would
be able to do so. There's a trove of information online: AntWeb.
org, AntWiki.org, and the Encyclopedia of Life (eol.org) all
have detailed pictures of just about every known ant. After
perusing the well-magnified and perfectly lit creatures pictured
by my various guides, I would turn back to the tiny insects
dashing around under my magnifying glass and rub my eyes. I
had no clue.

One problem was that there are thousands upon thousands of known ant species, and even more unknown species. Trying to find a match was like trying to find an identical grain of sand on a beach. I suspected I had something I hadn't heard of before, something that might shun cookies.

One of the best tools for identifying any species is a dichotomous key, which provides a series of either-or choices (for example, a dichotomous key for trees starts by asking, "Are you are looking at needles or leaves?") to lead you down a narrowing path, like the game Twenty Questions, until you reach the correct identification. But there are more than 350 dichotomous keys listed on AntWiki alone. These have titles like: "Key to Myrmica inezae species group." I needed a dichotomous key to the dichotomous keys!

Another problem was that my ants were so small. From the human perspective, an ant is pretty much just an ant. As soon as you begin to look at ants through a magnifying glass, however, a world of wonderful diversity snaps into focus. With the benefit of magnification, Wilson and Hölldobler write, ants "differ among themselves as much as do elephants, tigers, and mice. In size alone the variation is spectacular. An entire colony of the smallest ants . . . could live comfortably inside the head capsule of a soldier of the largest species, the giant Bornean carpenter ant, *Camponotus gigas*."

I'd ordered a hand lens online, a high-quality jeweler's loupe with tenfold magnification. As luck would have it, it arrived by mail later that afternoon. Using the lens took some getting used to, and I found it was impossible to catch the speedy ants in its narrow field of focus.

Eventually I realized that I'd never be able to identify my ants on the hoof. I plucked one out of the jar—stricken by guilt for a moment for leaving the other ant alone—and dropped it into a pool of rubbing alcohol. It stilled immediately. I fished it out with a pair of tweezers, repositioned my light, and bent over it with my hand lens.

There's something miraculous about a good magnifying glass. I squinted into a blurry mishmash of color, then pinpointed the correct focal distance and I found myself in a different world. When I'd been watching the insects in the grass with Josephine, I'd fancied it was something like a real-life version of Tolkien's Mirkwood—a forest filled with monsters. I'd loomed over the forest, separated by my bulk. But by bending light, the hand lens was able to transport me into that world: I was no longer peering down from above, but eyeball to antenna with one of the monsters. The ant was a great sodden beast splayed on an endless plain of woody cells—my bamboo desktop as I'd never seen it before.

The first thing you are supposed to do when trying to identify an ant is to look to see if it has one petiole or two. If you draw an ant, you'll likely start with three dots: the head, the thorax (the base for its six legs), and the abdomen (also known as the gaster). The petiole is a little lump (or a double lump) at the ant's waist, between the thorax and abdomen, and it was quite obvious in the photos I'd found online. When I looked through my hand lens, however, the petiole was nowhere to be found. In fact, I wasn't even sure my ant was right-side up. I took a breath, pulled the light down closer, and slowly began to find my bearings.

It took a good half hour of frustrating concentration and ungainly prodding with the tweezers, which appeared, in this magnified world, like rough-hewn steel girders. There's a peculiarity of the mind, or at least of mine, that presents tangible resistance to seeing something new. I had no system of categorization or naming to make sense of what I was seeing, and so for the first few minutes I saw nothing but a chaotic jumble of legs and body parts. I would stare at the images on my computer screen, then bend over and search for something similar on my ant. Eventually I found one landmark, then another.

I had thought this ant was black, but actually it was a translucent brown, with a darker, striped abdomen. It was beautiful, actually. I followed the curve of the head, found the antennae mounted about where you'd expect a nose, and to each side a black, multifaceted eye that was perfectly symmetrical, as if shaped by a jeweler from jet. I felt a shiver of delight. The eye of an ant! I'd seen thousands of ants, but until that moment, I hadn't realized I'd never seen one of their eyes. I felt richer for having seen it.

By nudging the ant's body to form a curve, I was able to expose the place where the petiole was supposed to be—and yes! There it was, nestled up against the abdomen, and there was very clearly just one. I'd found a simple dichotomous key for California house ants that walked me through a process of elimination starting with the question "One petiole or two?" A few steps later, the guide indicated that I was looking at *Linepithema humile*. I felt a chill of disappointment. This was not some interesting new species, it was the most common thing possible: an Argentine ant.

The Argentine Empire

Though common, the Argentine ant is also strange. Actually, the thing that makes it common is what makes it so interesting. There is just one species of the *Linepithema* genus in North America, and for a long time, there was just one colony—one massive imperial family. In most ant species, each colony is independent. Each lives for as long as the queen lives—fifteen, twenty-five years sometimes—then dies. When the queen reaches the end of her life the workers continue collecting food for a while, but the nurseries empty, and eventually there are no workers to replace the fallen. A colony without a queen is like a headless chicken: still running, but going absolutely nowhere.

Argentine ants, in contrast, produce multiple queens that generally stick around the nest. So instead of dying when the queen dies, an Argentine ant colony can grow in sprawling immortality. In a fit of creativity, scientists named the biggest one the Very Large Colony. In the summer of 1998, Neil Tsutsui and Andy Suarez, both grad students at UC San Diego, decided to see how big this Very Large Colony was. They collected some ants around San Diego, put them in jars, and drove north. They knew that ants from a different colony would fight with the ants they were carrying, but all the local ants they put in a jar with the ants they'd brought with them got along happily with the out-of-towners. Tsutsui and Suarez found that there was just one family of Argentine ants from beyond the Mexican border up through California to Ukiah, in Mendocino County. It was a single supercolony six hundred miles long.

That turned out to be just the beginning. On the West Coast, the ants made their way up to Vancouver Island, and scientists began asking, Where else? When they plopped ants from California and Japan in the same jar, the ants again recognized each other as colony mates. Same with ants from the Pacific Islands, Australia, New Zealand, South Africa, and Mediterranean Europe. The sun never sets on the Very Large Colony; it exists anywhere with the Mediterranean climate that Argentine ants love.

Most other species of ant are not as aggressively expansive as the Argentines. Colonies frequently squabble over borders, but manage to live side by side. Even ants that enslave other species don't entirely wipe out their adversaries. Argentine ants, on the other hand, simply overrun other colonies. They aren't built for war—they don't have the fancy weaponry that some other species have—but they are able to overwhelm their competitors by virtue of their numbers and efficiency. They take up all the territory and gobble up all the food. Some ants eat mostly meat, some ants need mostly sugar, but Argentine ants eat everything. As a result, the native ants have been wiped out wherever the Very Large Colony dominates. It wasn't just chance that my backyard ants were *L. humile*. In fact, it would have been surprising if I'd found anything else.

Perhaps the greatest advantage held by Argentine ants is that they thrive in the habitats created by modern humans. *L. humile* comes from the banks of the Rio Paraná, which frequently floods, tossing up massive piles of driftwood and mud, then washing them away just as quickly. The Argentine ants work with this constant change. They might form a nest under a rotting log until that location gets too wet, and then move the larvae uphill, under some leaves. Then they'll shift the nest yet again to be closer to a delicious rotting fish—all in one day. Urban and suburban lawns are the California versions of the Rio Paraná: landscapes that are regularly flooded by sprinklers, raked clean of leaves and sticks, and shorn of shaggy growth by mowers. Any species that wants to survive in this shifting environment has to be adaptable, and ready to abandon a home at a moment's notice.

Humans alter the natural landscape by building and gardening, and then Argentine ants move in and alter it still more: They raise herds of aphids and scale insects, which thrive on our rosebushes and fruit trees. They evict native ants, and by extension, native plants like the California bush poppy, which relies on harvester ants to distribute its seeds.

Argentine ants seem inexorable, but they are not on their way to global domination. It's more likely that we are now watching the decline and fall of their empire. The Very Large Colony is essentially one happy family, but other colonies are following it around the globe, and when these unfamiliar ants meet, they fight. Four colonies of Argentine ants are battling it out in Southern California now, keeping each other in check. And there are multiple colonies all along the Gulf Coast, showing up as far north as New Hampshire on the East Coast (which makes sense, because the bulk of the shipping traffic from Argentina goes to the southeastern United States). It's only a matter of time until more families of Argentine ants begin competing with the Very Large Colony, or until the colony breaks into warring factions. And then there are challengers among other species of immigrating ants, such as the red imported fire ant, the Asian needle ant, and the crazy ant, each of which appears to be wiping out its predecessors.

Perhaps the most significant threat to the Very Large Colony is its own success. It has created an international group of ants that recognize each other because they are so genetically similar. That lack of diversity is its Achilles' heel; it makes the entire empire susceptible to the same pathogens. Argentine ants abruptly vanished from a few blocks in the California cities of Riverside, San Diego, and Davis. Perhaps they were wiped out by insecticide treatment, but Philip Ward, a UC Davis ant scientist, favors another hypothesis: "Some pathogen has spread locally, causing population declines, a sort of colony collapse disorder for Argentine ants," he suggested. In New Zealand, Argentine ants were spreading like a tsunami throughout the 1990s, but by 2011 researchers found that the species had undergone a "catastrophic collapse" and native species were resurgent. Change is the only constant in nature.

In Defense of Invasion

The story we generally tell about invasive species is one of domination and extinction. A new species is always an invading army of ruthless totalitarians, replacing diversity and color with uniformity, leaving the world poorer. But this dire vision doesn't hold up to scrutiny.

Invaders get a lot of attention at first, when they look like they might be an existential threat. But journalists and scientists pay much less attention to what happens once they settle in to an environment. Environmental journalist Fred Pearce noticed that he would write stories about the terror of some new invasive, but then the furor would pass and no one would follow up to see what eventually happened. One of those stories was about a "killer algae," *Caulerpa taxifolia,* that was smothering the shores of the French Riviera and spreading through the Mediterranean. But when Pearce went back to check, he learned that soon after his piece was published the algae began to disappear. "They are now virtually gone," he wrote. "Nobody reported that. Not even scientists."

Another time, Pearce wrote about the zebra mussel, which overtook the Great Lakes, outcompeting native species for plankton and clogging pipes. People were fascinated by stories of the invasion. But the media wasn't interested in reporting that zebra mussels were only thriving because the lakes were so polluted. Zebra mussels eat the polluting algae, and in the long run have probably done more good than harm. Pearce writes, "Light penetrating through the water has revived plants on the lake bed, and many fish—like the previously endangered lake sturgeon and smallmouth bass—have done very well by eating zebra mussels."

"A lot of studies happen when a new species arrives, but people don't often go back to do follow-ups," said Eleanor Spicer Rice, a scientist who documented the way Asian needle ants displaced their Argentine ant predecessors in Raleigh, North Carolina. One study provides a snapshot of the disruption, but we often simply don't know what happens as the flux settles down.

When scientists *have* gone back to follow up, they have never found that the new arrivals created a single-species wasteland. The native species might not be present in the same abundance, might not be in the same places, but they are there. For instance, a study in 2000 suggested that the number of Blainville's horned lizards had declined by more than 50 percent in areas dominated by Argentine ants. These California lizards eat ants, but for some reason they don't thrive on a diet of Argentine ants. But then another study in 2013 found that the lizards were doing all right, and still occupying 75 percent of their 1989 range. Basically, the researchers found them everywhere except the places where people had built houses and shopping centers.

When I first heard about the Argentine ant invasion it sounded like a catastrophe, with them spreading implacably around the world. And they do spread, wiping out other ants and the lizards that eat them, but only within a narrowly defined habitat that allows them to thrive. That habitat just happens to be the one created by human development. Instead of saying that Argentine ants are spreading out of control, it would be more accurate to say they are simply a symptom of our presence.

Immigrant species often do reduce native populations, sometimes significantly. But the ecologist Mark Davis has pointed out that they rarely cause extinctions, and when they do it's of populations in isolated habitats like lakes or islands. All this mixing may yield more biodiversity by producing more combinations, hybridization, and new species. *Centaurea* plants introduced into California from Spain have evolved so much in their new habitat that they can no longer reproduce with the old-world species. Is this, asks conservation biologist Chris Thomas, now a California native plant?

And then there are cases in which invasive species have provided food or habitat for threatened natives. The gall wasps, for example, that spread into England with turkey oaks were lifesavers for the native birds of Britain (the young of the birds, affected by climate change, had started hatching before the caterpillars they eat emerged from their pupae). In Puerto Rico, the once-endangered coquí frog has rebounded in new forest habitat made up of nonnative trees.

There's no doubt that these immigrants change our environment, sometimes drastically. As human movement has stirred the worldwide biological stew, aggressive species have wiped out humble ones that had previously survived in some secluded corner. But nature thrives on change. Disturbance and mixing spur evolution, and scientists are finding many new species and hybrids arising with migration. On balance, it seems, the result of ecological immigration isn't gray uniformity, but just the opposite: Naturalizing species have given us richer biodiversity.

House Pets

A month after our pecan sandies adventure, the temperature dropped and the rain began to fall. Argentine ants generally stop foraging when the temperature drops below 41°F, so it was no surprise that they began to forage in the one place where it was still dry and warm—our kitchen. This gave me plenty of time to observe their behavior and look for clues to my mystery (why weren't they interested in pecan sandies?). The ants came streaming in, hunting out forgotten crumbs in the cupboard, infesting the trash can under the sink, and gorging on the sugar high up on a shelf. Some of my research proved useful during these invasions: Instead sweeping away the ants immediately, I carefully traced their trail to its destination and removed the food source. *Then* I'd wipe the ants away with a sponge. I felt a little ridiculous as I washed hundreds of crushed bodies off my hands when I recalled that I'd experienced a moral tremor upon drowning a single ant from the camellia.

On several subsequent days I noticed that the ants were nosing around a narrow crack between the butcher-block counter and the cupboard. The crack was just slightly wider than the body of an ant, and I wondered if they might be scouting it out as a new home. Then one night I saw that the countertop was thick with ants, all hurrying toward this crack. Looking closer, I saw that one of the ants was twice the size of the rest. I deftly captured it. Some species of ants produce workers of varying sizes that belong to different castes and can more efficiently perform certain tasks, such as defending the colony, but a quick Internet search confirmed that Argentine ants have only two types: workers and queens. The colony visiting my house was attempting to start a new stronghold inside my kitchen, and I had caught the queen. I sealed up the crack in my counter.

In the weeks that followed I caught half a dozen more queens. I kept one in a jar on my desk in the hope that I might see it lay eggs. But raising tiny pets can be difficult: Beth put that particular ant farm in the dishwasher without noticing there was anything inside.

The ants were implacable. No matter how careful we were to clean up our messes and lock away everything they might like, they always were able to locate some new food source. When we left the house for a week, I hoped we'd come back to discover the discouraged ants had left. Instead, they'd found their way inside a box of spice cookies I'd enclosed in not one, but two plastic bags. At that point, we broke down and bought traps containing ant food spiked with insecticide.

The ants ignored these traps in the same way they had ignored the pecan sandies. For all my research, I still hadn't figured out why my Argentine ants hadn't been interested in the cookies. But as I watched them in my kitchen, I saw that the ants would frequently become fixated on one particular food and walk past all others. It was like the movement of a crowd: If a great mass is pushing in one direction, it's very hard for one member of the crowd to stop it or change its course. The colony's interest in any particular goal grew organically, I speculated, from an initial discovery at just the right time, when there weren't other options competing for attention. Putting out the traps was a little like trying to get a convoy of people headed for a concert to take a detour to a baseball game instead.

When I asked Spicer Rice about my theory, she confirmed that I was finally on the right track. A colony will often focus on one thing at a time, she said. If ants are gathering water, they will keep going until a forager tries to put her water in the mouth of an ant in the nest but finds that that ant is already tanked up. The same is true with food. "They go out and get protein until they are full, and then switch and get sugar," she said.

We kept the kitchen cleaner than we've ever managed to before and eventually the ants disappeared. Either they found the traps, or they simply moved back outside after the rains stopped and the ground dried out.

After the Argentine ants disappeared, Beth mentioned that she'd seen another species in our kitchen. I was incredulous. Beth shrugged, "Well, maybe they were queens," she said. "But they did look different."

A few days later I spotted one of these ants. It was a bit darker than the Argentines, and its abdomen was big and round; it looked like it had an enormous butt. I nabbed it and dropped it into my specimen jar. But I was busy with other things and forgot about it.

A couple of months later, when I called Spicer Rice to ask about something completely different, she happened to mention that winter ants can live in tandem with Argentine ants. As soon as I hung up the phone, I fished my quarry out of the jar and bent over it with my lens. Again it took me a while to find the correct angle and focus, but when I did, it was clear that my ant had the distinctive hourglass thorax and swollen posterior of a winter ant.

Spicer Rice calls winter ants the white rabbits of the ant world, because they disappear down their holes into another world. Their tunnels may go twelve feet underground, the human equivalent of digging a mile deep. In the spring they disappear down these shafts and wait out the warm season underground. In the temperate Mediterranean climate where I live, Argentine ants dominate for most of the year, but they slow down in the coldest part of winter. Then the winter ants emerge and forage madly for food. As they eat, those already significant posteriors expand like balloons until they are stretched so thin that light passes from one side to the other. Then, their gasters full of fat, they return to the depths and seal the entrance for another year.

HIVE MIND

In his book *Adventures among Ants*, the ant scientist Mark Moffett suggests four ways of looking at an ant: as an individual, a selfless suffering drudge (the satirical newspaper *The Onion* once characterized ant farms as "the fun way to teach your kids to accept their miserable fate stoically"); as a society admirable in its organization; as an organism, a single body of many pieces; and, finally, as a mind, with intelligence arising from a crowd of simple choices.

This last metaphor, the colony as a mind, struck me when I read about research revealing how ants lay down chemical markers at a fork in a path to point their sisters toward the most fruitful direction. Each worker pauses at this decision point to make her sign pointing one way or the other. The following ants reinforce or contradict this sign, so the traffic on the network nimbly adjusts as conditions change. If there is a need for workers to haul a grasshopper home, the signals will point them in that direction. If invaders are approaching, the signals will direct workers more urgently to the battlefront. This fluid processing of complex information with a simple series of either-or decisions is similar to the binary system that drives computer science. And those forking paths aren't so different from neural pathways in the brain. Humans are more sophisticated thinkers than ant colonies. Then again, sometimes it feels like we would be better off with less sophistication. What is life but a series of trail bifurcations anyway? Perhaps the decisions we agonize over are, in fact, predetermined—the sums of a million individual cellular choices. Our conscious minds assume that we are in control, but often the role of consciousness is simply to justify and explain decisions over which it has no control. Are consciousness and reason just things evolution trumped up to keep us from going insane, a *Matrix*-style fantasy world that keeps us from recognizing the horrific reality that we have no agency and all the perseverating we do over choices is really just rationalization to convince ourselves that we have free will? Or, to flip the comparison around, could an ant colony develop consciousness? Feelings? Spirituality? Crumble some pecan sandies on a notecard with your daughter and eventually you end up grappling with the basic tenets of philosophy. These are the questions that arise if you spend enough time staring at ants.

CROW

FROM THE BEGINNING, I KNEW that I wouldn't necessarily succeed in imposing my enthusiasm for neighborhood nature on my daughter, and that my efforts might backfire. So, when Josephine became fascinated with the color pink, told me that my squirrel-spying walks were a little boring, and wanted to talk most of the time about what it meant to be a girl, I wasn't too disappointed.

"When I grow up I'm going to be a fairy, princess, ballerina," she would tell me.

I couldn't resist subtly slipping in "scientist" at the end of that litany, but I never pushed it any further than that.

By the time I had decided I needed to take a closer look at crows, Josephine was in full-throttle fairy-princess-ballerina mode and totally uninterested in the birds. That was all right, I decided. I never meant to force her to share my interests, I had just wanted to demonstrate to her, and to myself, that my non-human neighbors are important by paying attention to them.

It was the raptors that led me to crows. The story of the return of the raptors is fairly well known at this point: Ospreys and peregrine falcons were killed off in large numbers by organochlorine pesticides like DDT, but after use of these chemicals was restricted, they bounced back. These birds aren't invisible; some have adoring fans and webcams trained on their nests. Whenever I see the characteristic shape of a bird of prey, I look up eagerly. And it was in one of these moments that I began to see crows.

At first I assumed that both of the birds I was watching sail across the sky must be raptors. They crisscrossed my field of vision, disappeared behind the houses, then circled back. One was smaller and faster; the other was a red-tailed hawk, flapping ponderously. On the next pass there were two of the smaller birds. They were low enough now that I could see that they were black. The smaller birds weren't falcons or hawks, they were crows, and they were molesting the bigger bird mercilessly.

In San Francisco we lived at the foot of a tall, grassy hill—a good place, if you are a raptor, to find voles and other small rodents. I often saw hawks hunting there. I also saw crows ganging up on larger birds of prey. The crows made the bigger birds look positively clumsy. They'd swoop and turn in a fraction of the time it took the hawks to flap their wings. This behavior is called mobbing, but initially I could find no satisfactory explanation for why they do it.

Were the crows trying to keep the predator away from their nests? That seemed to make sense until I realized that I'd seen crows chasing hawks in the winter, when crows have no nests. The opposite could be true: The crows might be after the raptor's eggs. But why choose such dangerous food when there are pigeon eggs everywhere? That's like searching for tyrannosaurus eggs while surrounded by chickens. The crows, I learned, occasionally get just a bit too close to the birds of prey, which quickly kill them.

The crows may have been trying to steal something the bigger birds had killed. They do this sort of thing all the time, employing a two-crow con. Naturalists have observed one crow walking toward an eating eagle with feigned disinterest, just drifting closer nonchalantly. Then another crow will dash in from behind and pull the eagle's tail, causing it to leave its meal and give pursuit. The first crow darts in and snatches a piece of the kill, which it later shares with its accomplice.

None of these explanations, however, accounted for the fact that the crows I saw often harassed raptors for half an hour, maybe more. I would lose interest, carry on with my errands, then look skyward as I stepped out of a shop to see them still at it. You don't need that kind of time to steal a mouse.

I began to think of this differently after I read *Gifts of the Crow* by John Marzluff and writer and illustrator Tony Angell. Marzluff researches corvids—a family that includes crows and ravens—at the University of Washington, and he's written several books with Angell. They note that there's a direct evolutionary benefit to mobbing when it keeps predators from pillaging nests, but suggest that there's something more at work here. Mobbing looks a lot like a product of a culture, they write. "As a social exercise it provides a forum within which individuals can display their flight skills and aggressive tendencies. Not unlike the human recognition for a demonstration of valor, these attributes may win a daring crow a mate, or a higher rank in its avian hierarchy."

Among the Maasai, an adolescent boy used to have to kill a lion to earn his place in the patriarchy, and it's not so crazy to think that crows might earn status by challenging a larger predator.

Or maybe instead of earning status, they are just having fun: their version of extreme sports. Perhaps they do this aerial dance with death for the same reasons that humans do ostensibly pointless things like big-wave surfing or mountaineering. I like to imagine that crows are doing it out of sheer delight, for the joy of besting a force that could easily crush them.

That's not as fanciful as it sounds. Ravens have been observed "surfing" the wind by holding flat pieces of bark in their claws and riding mountain updrafts. They use bits of plastic to sled down snowy roofs, ride rotating sprinklers, and slide on their breasts down the onion-domed cupolas of Russian Orthodox churches (helpfully polishing them in the process). Angell and Marzluff once spotted an airborne group of crows playing with a ball of paper above a University of Washington football game. One crow would carry the ball a few wing lengths and then drop it, at which point the others would dive in, the fastest one snatching it from the air. They repeated rounds of this corvid quidditch over and over again, causing attention in the stands to stray from the earthbound athletes. And at the University of Montana, a crow learned to gather up small packs of dogs by whistling and calling what for all the world sounded like "Here, boy!" The bird would lead the dogs on frenzied chases across campus for no apparent reason.

To say that animals play strikes some as dangerously speculative. If you think of an animal as a Cartesian machine—a complex wetware robot that responds mechanically to a stimulus—it's hard to imagine why it would play. How could evolution tolerate frivolous risk and use of energy? But there's a clear scientific consensus: Animals do play, and crows are among the most playful.

"Many birds play," Angell and Marzluff wrote. "But no group of birds has been reported to play as frequently, as variably, or with as much complexity as the corvids."

This doesn't disprove the Cartesian argument, it only proves it's wrong in drawing a distinction between animals and humans. The more valid and interesting question is this: If we are all just complex machines designed to reproduce and pass on our DNA, why does anyone play?

People used to think that natural selection favors play when it provides valuable training; in crows, for example, mobbing might teach agility and build muscles. This makes intuitive sense, but scientists have found it doesn't work that way. Researchers have tested this out with mice, coyotes, kittens, squirrels, bears, and rats. They found that the individuals who played were no better at hunting or fighting than those who didn't. The behavioral ecologist Lynda Sharpe spent years watching meerkats tussle; to tell them apart during the rollicking melees, she had to sneak up to them as they napped and draw on them: "I'd crawl around the group on my stomach, clutching a fistful of marker pens and surreptitiously scribbling coloured rings on everyone's tails," she wrote. But after analyzing her data, Sharpe found that participating in this "training" had no relationship to success in real fights.

And yet, the play does do something: Research shows that animals that play are more likely to survive, and become better parents. Rats—one of the most playful species—that are deprived of play react to minor conflicts by flying into a rage or quaking in a corner.

"There's something about play that increases overall fitness, but it's not about hunting or fighting," said Kaeli Swift, a researcher who studies crows with Marzluff.

The definivite reasons for play are still mysterious. It's clear that play is simply fun; both crows and humans experience a flush of opioids in the brain when they play. But we don't know how this proximate cause of playfulness—the thrill of experiencing joy—leads to its ultimate cause, which is increasing reproductive fitness.

It's also clear that there's a social reason for playfulness. Play is a way of making meaning of the world. It provides an opportunity to act out aspirations (as children do in playing make-believe), reaffirm tribal unity (as fans do every day in stadiums around the world), and pass on a moral education for managing conflict. Perhaps mobbing is a dangerous ritual affirming the culture and solidarity of a crow clan.

THE CULTURAL MEMORY OF CROWS

Marzluff is probably most famous for showing that crows can recognize individual people. In 2002, he trapped a crow and slipped three plastic rings over its ankles—two light blue and one dark blue—to help him identify the bird. It turned out that this crow was Marzluff's neighbor, and whenever the bird saw him, it would caw wildly, castigating him and warning others that there was an evil crow grabber on the loose, one capable of inflicting his dubious fashion judgment upon his victims' ankles. This went on for more than seven years. Marzluff noticed that he always got this abuse no matter whether he was wearing a parka or a short-sleeved shirt, no matter whether he was alone or with a friend, no matter whether he was walking or driving his truck.

It seemed like the crow could recognize Marzluff's face, but of course it could have been something else: his scent, the curve of his shoulders, the particular cadence of his walk. So Marzluff bought a Halloween mask of a bald and bucktoothed caveman with a massive ledge of forehead hanging over the eyes and had his students wear it while capturing birds at the University of Washington. Sure enough, after that, whenever anyone wore the mask the crows would go crazy. Just to make sure they hadn't accidentally discovered that crows simply hate disguises, Marzluff got an even more terrifying mask—one that looked like former vice president Dick Cheney—and walked around campus with it on. The crows had no quarrel with Cheney, but continued to harass anyone who wore the caveman mask.

It was a tremendous feat to prove that crows recognize human faces, but what happened next was, to my mind, even more extraordinary. More and more crows flocked to scold the caveman, and some of these crows had no leg bands. "Not only was the crows' hatred of the caveman persistent," Marzluff wrote, "it was getting worse with time. . . . The number of birds scolding the caveman on a typical walk has increased threefold. And the vast majority of those who berate the Neanderthal were never even touched by him."

Crows were teaching each other to fear this bogeyman. This has been going on for eight years, and there's no sign they will forget the grudge. People who learn about this research are often captivated by the masks and fixate on the fact that crows can recognize individual people, Marzluff says. But the ability to see and remember visual markers in a face is a relatively simple cognitive task. Wasps, for instance, have it down pat: They identify one another by their facial markings. Dogs, monkeys, and pigeons can also recognize individual humans; so can sheep, honeybees, and even octopuses.

I think it seems strange to us because crows are doing something that we can't: differentiating the members of the other species. Most people can't differentiate individual crows. It's actually more correct to say that we *don't* recognize individual crows, instead of saying that we *can't*. Our face blindness is self-imposed, because we could see the differences between crows if we actually looked. After all, pet owners quickly learn to recognize their pets even when they're with others of the same breed.

To focus entirely on crows recognizing faces is to miss the most astonishing thing that Marzluff discovered: Fledglings learned to fear the caveman *in the abstract*. The young birds never actually saw the masked man capturing other crows, they had only seen their parents scold him. One generation passed the information to the next: *This momentous thing happened to our kind. Learn it. Never forget it. Teach your children.* This transmission of information is challenging enough that only the most intelligent creatures can manage it. It allows for the formation of tradition. In fact, it seems to me that if you take the same phenomenon and perpetuate it for thousands of years, you have something that looks very much like a religious observance. What are seders or the rituals of Christmas but means of perpetuating deep cultural memories? Perhaps those crows I saw mobbing red-tailed hawks were not showing off or playing, but instead reenacting an ancient ceremony so laden with meaning that I could not hope to understand it with simple evolutionary explanations.

Love, Hate, and Obsession

There's a clear evolutionary advantage in being able to differentiate one person from another when one of them will try to shoot you and the other will feed you peanuts. Crows use their facial recognition ability to torment those who cross them, and also to reward those who help them. They sometimes leave little gifts for friends. Angell and Marzluff report that on Valentine's Day of 2006, nature writer Gary Clark jokingly asked the crows he regularly fed why they never brought him anything in return. Later that day, when he returned to retrieve his feeding tray, he found a candy heart placed exactly in the center with LOVE printed on one side. Surely the timing of this gift—and the message it bore—was coincidental (no scientists think crows can read), but lots of people have received gifts from crows after feeding them.

Those who anger crows, on the other hand, suffer creative retribution. Carolee Caffrey, a zoologist at Oklahoma State, has described a crow expertly bombarding a student with pinecones. The student was climbing a tree to study the crow's nest, and the crow plucked three pinecones and dropped each on the student's head.

In another story collected by Angell and Marzluff, Seattle resident Gene Carter earned the ire of his neighborhood crows by scaring them away from a robin's nest. After that, a crow scolded him every morning and evening when it spotted him walking to and from his bus stop. The bird would dive toward him threateningly, "occasionally rapping him on the head, always amusing his wife and fellow commuters," they write. This went on for a year, until Gene moved to a new house. He was careful to move each load of his belongings to the new residence by a circuitous route to avoid being followed, immediately giving up and turning back if he saw a crow.

WHAT MAKES A CROW

I found that crows are a bit more difficult to observe carefully than some of the other species I'd begun to watch in writing this book. Crows are liable to fly off: They're not wedded to any one spot. And they are aware, and suspicious, of observers. When I watch them, they watch me. I don't need to take a single step toward a group of crows to arouse their vigilance, it's enough just to stop and stare at them instead of continuing with the flow of foot traffic. Pigeons are glad for human company and seek our patronage. Easily distracted squirrels quickly forget that you are there. To ants, we are incomprehensibly foreign. And to ginkgos our lives are insubstantial shadows, flitting past. But to crows, we are peers. They know better than to trust us, and unless there's good reason to share, they keep their secrets to themselves.

One soggy Sunday afternoon as Josephine and I walked to the grocery store, Josephine pointed out a pair of black shapes on a rooftop, their profiles sharp against the iron-gray sky. The crows were dipping their beaks into the roof's gutter and plucking something out, but it was impossible to see what it was with the naked eye.

They went about their work with the busy economy of motion of farmworkers harvesting a row of crops—though these farmworkers stopped every few seconds to watch the large carnivorous creatures who stood watching them. One crow fluttered to the next roof over and began working its gutter. I speculated aloud that there might be fat grubs living in the gutter leaf litter. Josephine suggested it was more likely that the crows were eating chocolates. Later, Swift would tell me that Josephine's guess might have been closer. She often uses Cheetos to gain crows' trust, and they love to hide these treats—and other food—in gutters.

The crows pecked busily. Then they flew away: darker wings against dark clouds.

The Blackness of Crows

The blackness of crows fairly radiates from their feathers, which impressed itself upon me when I took my lunch to a park one day. I found a seat near a pair of crows perched in a tree. One of the birds had a white streak on the underside of one of its tail feathers. I thought at first that this was a guano stain, but it didn't look like it: It was very pure white, not clumpy or streaked. When I checked into it later, I learned that many birds do indeed lack pigment in a few feathers.

I watched my white-streaked crow (and it watched me back) while I ate a quesadilla and wondered, *Why black?*

Lyanda Lynn Haupt, in her book *Crow Planet,* described crow colors in detail after she spent two full days staring at one on her desk (a stuffed scientific specimen) to see if she could open her eyes to something new. She noticed that the innermost half of breast feathers—the part usually covered by other feathers—was gray and explained, "It takes some biological effort to produce dark pigmentation, and if it is not needed because the feathers are not visible, then natural selection does away with it."

Basic pigmentation must be pretty cheap (biologically speaking), or else creatures without coloring or patterns would be everywhere. But I could imagine that producing that deep, silky blackness does demand more resources than gray does. You can glimpse the gray when the wind disturbs the breast of a crow.

If blackness is biologically expensive, what are crows (and blackbirds, and ravens) getting in return for paying this premium? Nobody knows for sure, but there seems to be a provisional consensus among ornithologists that the blackness allows the birds to be seen.

Many animals are patterned for camouflage: Any variation in color helps break up the profile of the creature. If a tiger is creeping up on me through the jungle, for instance, instead of seeing a solid block of orange in the shape of a tiger, I'll see stripes of orange and black, which would be easy to misinterpret as branches, shadows, and shafts of light. Pure black, on the other hand, stands out against almost all of nature's backgrounds. There's no misinterpreting the shape when it's all one color. This visibility is helpful for social birds like crows because it allows members of a group to see each other clearly. An individual crow is puny, but a murder of crows can chase off eagles—and drive grown men to change their addresses.

Even an all-black dress code can contain further complexities. After staring at her crow for hours, Haupt noticed that "the black glossy feathers on the crown and back are outlined with iridescent violet, giving them a scaled appearance." This contrasts with the feathers on the back of the neck, which are flat black. The small body feathers, Haupt wrote, are "as soft as rabbit fur," while the wing and tail feathers are stiff.

Ravens and Crows

Here is how I try to tell if I'm looking at a raven or a crow. If the bird is flying, I look at the tail. Crows have a rounded fan. Ravens have a diamond-shaped tail. I also watch the bird closely when it lands. Ravens are quiet and still. Crows fidget and complain. Their voices are different, too. Crows "caw" abrasively. Ravens "rawk" in the pebbled baritone of a woman who has tended a smoky bar for thirty years.

Once I have a pretty good idea, I look for other features to confirm. Ravens are bigger, and they have thicker beaks and a luxurious beard of feathers on the neck. Crows are slimmer: gracile, sleek. The average raven is two and a half pounds to the crow's one pound, but it's hard to judge that unless you have the two side by side. Really, though, I identify crows mostly by knowing that ravens are rarer in my neighborhood, so any big black bird I see is probably a crow.

Ravens live just about everywhere on Earth, from deserts to

the soggy northwestern coast of America. Crows are a little more particular: They like to be near people. In fact the Asian house crow seems to live *only* in the company of humans. You could call them obligate synanthropes: They depend on us for their habitat.

Crows do well in the landscapes we create. They like farms, from which they pilfer grain. They like lawns, where they find worms and crane flies. They like bird feeders and bags of garbage and roadkill. Humans supply it all.

CORVID BOOM

One winter, the online news organ in my town, Berkeleyside.com, ran an article on the local multiplication of crows. People had noticed, with some alarm, that every year there were more of them. When the Audubon Society conducted its annual bird counts in the 1980s, there were always fewer than a hundred crows tallied, and just a handful of ravens. After 2010, the birders were regularly counting more than a thousand crows, and as many as three hundred ravens. There are reports that the same is true in other cities.

I hadn't lived in the area long enough to witness the increase myself, but I had noticed the crows out in force. When I run in the park every morning, there are always small groups of black figures patrolling the grass. Every once in a while I'll follow a bird's line of flight to a tree harboring dozens of crows.

People were worried that the crows must have come at the expense of biodiversity. Crows sometimes rob the nests of other birds to eat the eggs and chicks. Would the increase in crows lead to a crash in songbird populations?

Kevin McGowan, a corvid researcher at the Cornell Laboratory of Ornithology, said that wasn't likely. When researchers put cameras on nests to catch robbers, they found that the culprits usually weren't crows, they were squirrels or snakes. Crows, McGowan told Berkeleyside, "are way down on the list," behind raccoons, raptors, opossums, and jays.

Eventually, if the population of crows grows large enough, it can affect the system, Marzluff told me. But the birds that feel the impact also thrive around humans, like robins and jays. The threat to biodiversity comes not from crows, but from humans making drastic changes to habitats. Furthermore, people have tried getting rid of crows, and scientists have watched to see if it helps other birds. To put the findings simply: It just doesn't work.

I suspect that the dismay accompanying the rising number of crows stems from the sense that every addition to the natural world results in some equal and opposite subtraction. Crows are humanlike in their creativity and their ability to thrive in the ecosystems we shape, so their presence looks to some observers like an extension of human disruption. We lay waste to the earth, and then crows take advantage of the changes and elbow their way in. From this perspective, the booming crow populations look like diminishments of nature.

The evidence, however, doesn't support this fear. In 2012, ornithologists at UC Berkeley dug up dusty bird surveys dating back to 1913 and compared what they reported with the species they saw on campus. They expected to see a decline, a steady fall from Eden, because so many buildings had gone up on campus, the surrounding area had changed from farms and pastures to an urban grid. But instead, the researchers found a small *increase* in bird diversity over the century.

Across North America, crow populations are increasing, though much more modestly than by the full order of magnitude seen in Berkeley and other cities. Meanwhile, overall bird diversity has stayed steady. In the United States, the Environmental Protection Agency found that 113 bird species have suffered significant declines in the last half century. But at the same time, 118 species have benefited from significant increases in numbers.

City Birds

There's one more question embedded in the observation that crow populations are increasing. That question is: Why are the biggest increases in cities?

The answers are slightly different across America. The American crow isn't endemic to the West Coast, it followed suburban developments across the United States, glorying in the irrigated lawns that turned the inhospitable West into ideal habitat. They reached the West Coast sometime around 1960, Marzluff said. Part of their increase in western cities is attributable to their colonization of new land.

In eastern North America the most likely explanation for booming urban crow populations is that they are moving from the countryside into towns. And we know with certainty that this is happening. By doing a little historical research, McGowan found that at least one roost had moved from three miles outside the town of Auburn, New York, in the 1930s to the middle of town. And many other cities—Pittsburgh, Albuquerque, Minneapolis, and Ottawa, Canada—have seen roosts develop.

A roost is a great congress of birds gathered for the night. Starlings and nuthatches also roost, as do robins, though in lesser numbers. Crows often roost together through the winter, then separate in the spring to build nests for eggs. These roosts can grow stupendously large. One, in Fort Cobb, Oklahoma, had around two million crows. McGowan describes standing beneath a roost of more than fifteen thousand crows in central Ohio and marveling at the volume of excrement underfoot. Crows, like many birds, swallow bits of rock to help break down the grain they eat, and McGowan estimated that the crows in that particular roost could drop 1,650 pounds of gravel around that tree every five months.

If there are more roosts moving into cities, then it stands to reason that crows are staying in towns during the day as well. But why have they moved?

Maybe it's because there are laws against firing guns within most cities. Now that we are no longer primarily agrarian and scarecrows are a symbol rather than a practical tool, we don't see crows as our enemies. And vice versa: Crows may have simply gotten more comfortable being surrounded by humans all the time. Marzluff notes that city crows tend to be much less skittish around people, and more likely to aggressively scold humans.

McGowan suggests that the move to cities might also have something to do with the invention of streetlights. Great horned owls are the most effective predator of crows, swooping in noiselessly from the dark to grab them. But few owls penetrate to the city centers, and with the glow from the streetlights, the crows have a chance to see them coming. (Crows, like most birds, can't see very well in the dark.)

McGowan also says that crows are roosting in cities because that's where the trees are. The grand old trees in parks and cemeteries are often the largest trees around, the only ones to survive the most intense period of logging and development. Since the early 1900s, urban forests have sprung up. If you look at pictures of American cities from a century ago, you'll find many streets were treeless. By foresting along the sidewalks, we've created a habitat that simply didn't exist before, a massive surface area composed of branches for nesting and perching. The leaves and berries, the insects that feed off them, and the spiders that eat those insects are all in turn the food for birds and other creatures.

I find all this tremendously heartening. Instead of being a symptom of human destruction, crows seem to be moving in because, at least for them, we are improving the habitat. In his book *Welcome to Subirdia,* Marzluff tells how he spent two weeks birding in Montana's Glacier National Park, then flew to New York and went out bird-watching in Central Park. He was surprised to discover that in New York, he saw a greater diversity of birds by midday than he had during his entire stay in Glacier National Park. The science supports his experience. Studies have found there is very low diversity in bird species at the concrete core of a city when there are no nearby parks. The biodiversity of remote woodlands is higher than that. But the greatest number of unique bird species can be found in cities that have big parks.

Human density can go hand in hand with biological diversity. Our civilization is not always a force desolating the earth.

That doesn't mean that those trying to preserve wilderness are misguided or that we should be building condos in Yosemite. We need remote areas to support all the species that don't thrive alongside humans. The point is that the places where people live, if thoughtfully designed, might also be places for the rest of creation to thrive.

Marzluff would like to see cities located near at least a hundred acres of dense forest, ideally consisting of native vegetation and abutting a waterway. Berkeley, for instance, which researchers found has a wide variety of species, borders a two thousand–acre wooded park.

I believe bringing people together with other species is beneficial, even for people who aren't nature lovers. Evidence shows that stress levels drop and health improves when people are in the company of plants and animals. If we care about biodiversity and want to experience it personally (in addition to knowing it exists somewhere else, thousands of miles away), it's eminently possible to increase the species richness of our daily lives by nurturing a variety of habitats in and around cities.

Flying Monkeys

Here's another potential explanation for the rise of crows in cities: More people make more crows. Marzluff estimates that the territory a nesting family of crows controls is about the size of two backyards. That's about one crow per person. This equation breaks down as density increases and backyards disappear under skyscrapers. But when a city is dominated by freestanding homes, an increase in population usually means more lawns and more garbage, and therefore more crows.

The attributes that allow crows to thrive in our company also make them interesting. They are innovative and flexible. They pay close attention to us, read our body language, and anticipate our intentions. Neuroscientists studying crows have shown that they can quickly and accurately infer the cause of an unexpected event. They also, like humans, can make mistakes about what causes what; in other words, crows can develop superstitions.

Sometimes they seem to toy with humans. Angell and Marzluff tell the story of a crow pilfering a sandwich from golfers and then returning the empty sandwich bag to them two holes later. Another pair of ravens stole a pie from sea kayakers, then bombed them with the pie tin the following day.

Crows use humans. They drop nuts and shellfish on roads to be smashed by our high-speed steel-belted radial nutcrackers. At certain intersections in Japan, it's common to see crows tossing nuts into the road, waiting for the signal, and then walking with the pedestrians to retrieve their reward.

The birds quickly adapt to our ways. In the 1950s, when cars started zipping down the highways, crows would fly away from the sides of the road whenever a vehicle passed. By the 1960s, they were barely flinching as cars zoomed by.

New Caledonian crows, which have the largest brains among crows, use and even make tools. For example, they carefully trim twigs into hooks to excise insects from tight cracks. Some behavioral ecologists were skeptical of the amazing feats reported to have been accomplished by New Caledonian crows until researchers filmed one, Betty, using tools to lift a basket of food out of a cylinder. It's an astonishing video. Betty first attempts to spear the food with a wire the researchers had provided. She considers a moment, then wedges a rod under a rock, deftly bends it into a hook, and fishes out the food. Betty does this nimbly, without a misstep. This video demonstrated that the crow is able to think three steps ahead: First, *Gosh, it sure would be a lot easier to get the food if this rod had a curved end;* second, *Maybe I could bend the rod to make a hook;* and third, *I could use that rock to bend the rod.* These birds are amazingly clever. To raise the bar, researchers devised an experiment in which the crow would have to pull up a string to retrieve a short stick, then use that stick to retrieve a longer stick, and then use the longer stick to get a piece of meat. The crow did it on the first try.

American crows are not as clever as New Caledonian crows, but they are still very smart. Researchers compare their level of intelligence to that of primates. "They're like little flying monkeys," Marzluff said.

Using Crows as Crows Use Us

In at least one way, though, American crows are considerably more resourceful than humans. Crows have exercised their considerable intelligence to exploit human quirks—our wastefulness with food, our reflexive desire to carpet outdoor spaces with grass, our predictable driving habits—but humans have devoted no thought to how we might take advantage of the rise of crows in our midst. Why are we the stupid ones in this relationship?

This question has obsessed Josh Klein for nearly a decade. Klein is one of those Information-Age Renaissance men who not only ponder crazy ideas, but also take the process a step further by engineering those ideas into existence. Klein's ideas for making the relationship between humans and crows more reciprocal began in the form of a vending machine: He built a box designed to produce a peanut every time a crow inserted a coin. Then, working with a crow trainer, he demonstrated that the birds could learn how to find coins and exchange them for food.

When people hear about his crow box, Klein says, many tell him he's going to get rich. He's not optimistic about making money; he just wants to make the relationship between humans and crows a mutually beneficial one. He's disturbed by the fact that very few people have noticed that some animals have changed to thrive with modern humanity. It's not just crows, but raccoons, rats, deer, turkeys—by some estimates these species have larger populations than ever existed in North America before. "We have these animal populations evolving to take advantage of us," Klein told me. "We can't kill them off. And we aren't doing anything to make it a more productive relationship. We are effectively breeding them for parasitism. I think it could be disastrous."

The crow box is Klein's contribution toward establishing a more balanced relationship. When I spoke to him, Klein said that he was redesigning the crow box because it had proved too difficult for some of the beta testers. I assumed that by "beta testers" he meant the crows and asked what it was about his machine that had been hard for them. He quickly corrected me: The crows were doing fine, the problematic beta testers were humans who had struggled to set up the machines. "Asking what about the crow box makes it hard for crows is like asking, 'What about your front door makes it hard for your teenage son to use?'" he said. It's clear that crows can work the vending machine; tame birds were ready to exchange money for peanuts after watching Klein set it up and test the box. But just because a teenage boy knows how to operate a front door doesn't mean he's going to be interested in coming home every night for a family dinner.

For crows, the mechanics were easy, motivation was much more complicated. After one crow learned how to work the vending machine, it began to hide the coins rather than inserting them for peanuts. Instead of being compelled to action by a reward of a peanut, it seemed to be compelled to watch the spectacle of its human colleagues searching furiously for the coins. Another time, Klein was training a crow using raw hamburger—to a crow, a more enticing reward than peanuts. While no one was watching, the crow hid some of the meat in Klein's jacket pocket.

"When I was getting ready to go I put on my jacket, put my hand in my pocket, and screamed like a little girl," he said. "The owner of the crow laughed his ass off, and the crow—they make this *caw-aw-aw* call that sounds like laughing."

The very next time they met for a training session the crow snuck into the bathroom, stole some toilet paper, wet it in the toilet water, and cached it in Klein's jacket pocket. When Klein put on his jacket and felt the wet mass, he jumped again, then gaped at the complexity of the practical joke.

There's no doubt that crows can operate Klein's vending machines if they want to, but it may turn out that they simply find it more entertaining to live off human excess than to work for peanuts. Whatever ends up happening with this project, in my opinion, it's already a success. No matter how efficiently it hacks the behavior of crows, it has already hacked the behavior of humans. Klein gets e-mails weekly from people who have heard about the crow box and want to know more. It's snapped people out of their normal pattern of ignoring animals until they become a problem that can no longer be ignored. Klein is not going to single-handedly put us on a path to coevolutionary harmony with crows, but I do think he's taken the right first step by replacing ignorance with curiosity and attention.

FAMILY LIFE

Though I've been looking, I haven't managed to find a crow's nest. They prefer conifers, Marzluff told me, because evergreens provide year-round cover. It's apparently easy to mistake a squirrel's nest for a crow's nest. "Actually, squirrels' nests typically start off as crows' nests," Marzluff said. But squirrels like to use leaves and pine needles, and crows prefer sticks. In addition, crows use grass whereas squirrels don't, so McGowan looks for grass sticking out of the bottom of a nest.

In the spring, a mated pair will lay down a crosshatch of sticks (although in Tokyo, where coat hangers are more abundant than sticks, crows sometimes use those instead). Then they'll add mud and grass. Finally, the female will line the nest with some soft and comfortable material.

Sometimes the offspring born the previous year will help with nest building. They stick around until they reach sexual maturity between the ages of two and four. Crows are different from most other birds in that the males sometimes stay even longer than that, until well after they are capable of starting their own families (the females, in contrast, always leave). They assist with feeding the next generations and cleaning up the nest.

The eggs range from sky blue to aquamarine, and are flecked with brown. Crows keep the nests clean by tossing out the chicks' scat until they grow large enough to poop over the edge.

The chicks are ridiculous. They slump in the bottom of the nest as if they are dead, like sagging black assemblages of skin and delicate bone. But then, whenever there is a noise—a passing car, say, or a barking dog—they spring up like jack-in-the-boxes and open their mouths so wide that they all but disappear behind their straining red maws. As they age, the insides of their mouths darken and are fully black by the time they reach sexual maturity. If you think you might be looking at a juvenile, watch until it opens its mouth.

HINTS OF CULTURE

As soon as I started learning about crows, I began seeing them everywhere. It was almost as if all I needed to do was muse for a moment about some aspect of crow behavior to make one appear. But I had been unsuccessful in my attempts to eavesdrop on the more intimate aspects of their lives, and I certainly haven't found much that would capture the curiosity of my three-year-old. No crow family has claimed my backyard as its territory, and the nests nearby must be well hidden, because I haven't spotted any. Whenever I can, I stop to watch crows, but they quickly notice me watching them. *Why is this human staring at us?* I imagine them thinking, and then they wing away. Usually humans are blind to crows, and when we do pay close attention to them, they've learned that it often portends violence.

Nonetheless, I have managed to notice a few things I hadn't seen before. For example, crows are almost always in pairs. They aren't always side by side, though; they split and regroup, then split again. When they lose visual contact, they call back and forth until they are reunited. If the crows continue these calls, other crows also come. This gathering call is the classic *caw-caw* that you probably associate with crows. The scolding that accompanies the mobbing of a raptor has a harsher, screaming tone. Crows are said to have different warning calls for humans and raptors, but I haven't been able to tune my ear to the difference. They make other sounds too: a clicking trill that sounds like a spoon rattling over a washboard, a bell-like chiming. Swift has recorded a two-toned moan, a rising minor second that sounds just like the famous half step in *Jaws: duuh*-duh, *duuh*-duh. No one knows what these sounds mean, and it seems likely to me, given the other similarities between crows and humans, that they mean different things in different places, depending on the local dialect. We know that each flock of crows has its own set of calls forming a sort of song. If an outsider is trying to join a flock and sings the wrong song, the group attacks. But sometimes outsiders stick around long enough to learn the group's song, which, just as is often the case in human tribes, leads to acceptance.

Most of crow culture is inconspicuous, and they seem to like it that way, but a crow funeral is striking. It's a sight strange enough to snap normally crow-blind adults out of their spells. When the birds come across a dead body of their own kind, they call in their neighbors. This can go on until a giant congregation is present. Scientists have observed crows placing objects near bodies, and even outlining them with sticks. Haupt has also witnessed what she called a "crow hospice"—a silent gathering around a bird that was dying.

Kaeli Swift is studying these funerals by laying a taxidermied crow on the ground. Each time the pair of crows that controls the territory sees this dead bird, they call their neighbors. Sometimes just a handful show up, Swift said, sometimes forty-five birds have come. They scream, then go quiet, then all scream again. It usually lasts for about twenty minutes. But Swift cautions that what she sees may be different from authentic funerals because she is introducing an unknown bird. "There might be a significant distinction between a stranger bird and a mate of ten years," she said. For instance, Swift didn't see any crows holding silent vigils, but there are credible documented observations of crows assembling noiselessly around the body of a compatriot.

Swift has proposed several possible explanations for the behavior. The first is that the crows come to study the cause of death and learn how to avoid it themselves. Avoiding death, along with successful reproduction, is an evolutionary driver powerful enough to create all sorts of behaviors. I have a pet theory that the human fascination with narrative grew from this evolutionary seed: The simplest, most gripping stories tend to be ones about narrowly avoiding death or finding love. So perhaps crows are storing away the lessons death and dying offer so they can pass them on to their chicks.

The second explanation is that these gatherings are less funerals than readings of the will. The death shakes the social hierarchy and the crows assemble to see what it means: Is a mate newly available? Is there territory to be claimed? Perhaps they watch each other and assess who is going to make the first move.

The other possible explanations are emotional rather than rational: The crows gather to grieve or to engage in some kind of spiritual ceremony.

There's no reason that several of these possibilities can't all be correct. In fact, it makes perfect sense that emotional and rational explanations would go together, given what we know of neuroscience. The experiences that are stamped most firmly into the memory are the ones accompanied by a powerful limbic system response. Emotion is the glue that makes reason stick.

To many people, roosts of thousands of crows and crow funerals are eerie. When a crow appears in a movie, it's almost always an ominous symbol. But the influence of crows in our cultural heritage goes far beyond a gloomy omen. We recognize in these birds strange reflections of ourselves, and we gesture to these similarities to make meaning: You can find corvids embedded everywhere in our language. Marzluff and Angell point out that we have crowbars and crow's-feet, we rave and are ravenous, we "eat crow" and reckon distance "as the crow flies." These expressions suggest that crows and ravens might even have affected the way we think, because we've been using crow metaphors to explain the world for so long that they are now part of the bed-rock of collective memory.

I value the cultural associations we've made with crows and all the meaning we have built atop them. But it troubles me that we now understand the crow much better as a symbol than as a bird. We've used crows to enlighten our own culture, yet ignore their culture.

It's clear to me that crows do have culture. They pass on lessons to their children and compatriots. They play, and tease, and harbor grudges. They do things that seem illogical, implying deep and intricately reasoned motivations. Raptor mobbings and crow funerals suggest, at the very least, a keen, perhaps overactive, curiosity. At the very most they suggest culture: a collective, perhaps spiritual, affirmation of memory and community.

SNAIL

WHEN A FRIEND BROUGHT ELISABETH Tova Bailey a snail as a present, along with some field violets, she was perplexed and asked what purpose this creature was supposed to serve.

"I don't know. I thought you might enjoy it," was her friend's reply.

Bailey was bedridden by a rare illness, or perhaps by the drugs the doctors had given her to cure it, and she was in no position to take responsibility for a pet, let alone exert the will necessary to enjoy the company of a snail. But then the snail unfurled itself from its shell, slipped down the pot, and consumed a single purple petal from a withered blossom. As she watched, Bailey became aware that she could hear chewing, like the sound of a tiny person eating a tinier stick of celery.

So begins Bailey's beautiful, spare book, *The Sound of a Wild Snail Eating*. Bailey did enjoy her snail as her friend had hoped. Convalescence had reduced her to a snail's pace, but she found some small consolation in this diminishment of speed. Bailey, often too weak even to roll over in bed, fixed her attention on the mollusk living a few inches from her head and began to notice things that most of us never see or hear. She would even contribute to the scientific literature on snails, making the first observation of a snail caring for its own eggs. The aim of the book you are holding is to persuade people (myself first and foremost) to slow down enough to see the wonders around us. Bailey, on the other hand, forced to move slowly, had no choice but to cling to the observation of small things. She wrote, "Survival often depends on a specific focus: a relationship, a belief, or a hope balanced on the edge of possibility. Or something more ephemeral: the way the sun passes through the hard, seemingly impenetrable glass of a window and warms the blanket, or how the wind, invisible but for its wake, is so loud one can hear it through the insulated walls of a house." And so she trained her focus upon a snail.

THE JASMINE KINGDOM

I'd seen snails around my backyard on occasion. They appeared after rains, each about the size of a knuckle, waving their horns enthusiastically. I saw them most frequently in and around a thicket of jasmine growing at my back door. When I searched the deck beneath the jasmine, I saw that it was spotted with piles of scat. Josephine and I crouched down beneath the jasmine and looked closer. There were dozens of little turds, some draped in piles that seemed too large to have come from a snail.

"Ew," Josephine said.

Something shiny white was wedged between the planks. I tugged it free and found I was holding a shard of what must have been a massive snail shell. The interior was pearly, and curved into a perfect spiral. From this low vantage point, I could peer into the jungle of vines. There must be a whole society of snails in there, pruning my jasmine from the inside out. "Society" isn't too strong a word: Snails do communicate among themselves, and they coordinate their efforts. The USDA warned in a snail-farming newsletter that a team of gastropods imprisoned in a box can combine their muscular efforts to lift a heavy lid and escape. Crouching there, I marveled to have discovered a complex hidden world that had previously escaped my detection, though I walk by that very location several times every day.

A few hours of research taught me that the prodigious offerings on my porch were indeed snail poop. In my reading, I also came across a diagram of snail anatomy and was confused by the fact that the organ labeled "anus" seemed to be inside the shell. A little more digging confirmed that I was not misreading it: Snails poop on their own heads. Josephine laughed and laughed at this, but it doesn't seem to bother the snails. The droppings slide out and onto the ground. If snails destroy your garden, you can accurately call them shitheads.

This inconvenient arrangement of anatomy is an accident of evolution, living evidence of unintelligent design. A snail starts out upon hatching with its gut in a straight line: The mouth is at the front, the anus is at the rear. But as the shell grows into a spiral, the body twists along with it. A bit of food eaten by a snail travels upward through the gut toward the apex of the spiral, then back down again.

ARCHITECTURAL GEOMETRY

If you shrank to a centimeter and walked up into an unoccupied snail shell, you would find yourself in a smooth white tube turning upward like a spiral staircase. If, like most snails' shells, yours was dextral, you could run your left hand along the interior wall, the axis of the spiral. Turn around to face the opening, and you would see the passageway turning always to the right (*dexter* in Latin) as it opened. Some snails, however, are sinistral, with their spirals to the left, coiling clockwise. The orientation of a snail's architecture influences its sexuality. The sexual organs of two snails will properly align only when they have matching shells.

As you continued walking up into your shell, you would find the walls rapidly closing in on you until you were forced to stoop, then crawl. If you were not claustrophobic, you could lie down and reach your arm up around the next curve. On the way back, you would notice the diameter of the passageway increasing dramatically until it became an echoing hallway. The sound of each footstep would ricochet off the curving walls, up to the spire and back down again, until there was a sea of echoes that sounded like waves on a beach. These echoes are a product of the mathematical properties of the shell. Each shell is a perfect logarithmic spire. Though they vary spectacularly in size and color, and though the spiral may be as squat as a cinnamon roll, as they are in my garden snails, or drawn out like a conch's, every shell follows this geometric rule, its radius increasing exponentially as it opens outward. Mathematically, snail shells conform to the golden ratio, the value that biology employs hundreds of times in radial growth, and just the right pattern to grow spiral rings without creating a gap.

The shells grow, I learned, as snails exude minerals, which harden in place around the opening. Snails require an ample supply of calcium to build their homes, but calcium often is hard to find in forests and gardens. The snail, writes Bailey, "is the only known land animal able to find calcium by smell." And because the snail carries chemical receptors in each of its tentacles, it can smell in stereo. By waving its horns, it can sniff out the direction of the mineral's scent, and perhaps also gauge its distance. It also has retractable eyes at the tips of these "telescopic watch-towers," to borrow nineteenth-century physician James Weir Jr.'s description. Snails' eyesight is poor, able to detect light and movement but not much else. They taste with their lower tentacles. They have no sense of hearing. They experience the world mostly through touch and smell.

I ADOPT A SNAIL

I found a brown snail the size of a pencil eraser nestled beneath the curl of a pink camellia blossom. Inspired by Bailey, I picked the blossom and put it in a glass jar on my desk. I added half an eggshell for calcium and filled it with water. On that first night, the snail crept up from the flower onto the glass, affixed itself there, then retreated into its shell. In this position, I could examine it from every angle. My snail, like its relatives in the jasmine bush, was a brown garden snail, *Cornu aspersum,* the same species eaten in fancy restaurants. *Cornu* means horn-shaped, and *aspersum* means spattered, or strewn. Its shell was flecked with a dozen shades of brown, streaked with darker brown stripes parallel to its spiral. There was a new edge of shell, white and translucent, like a baby's fingernail, about a centimeter wide. I could see the shell from both inside and out, because the snail's foot was withdrawn deeply into the cavity, with a thin layer of slime around the edge of the shell gluing it to the glass. It stayed in this position day after day. The new shell growth darkened.

The pattern of concentric lines emerged in the white like an image on a slow-motion Polaroid, but the snail was otherwise motionless and unchanged.

In the face of inclement weather, irksome dryness, or disagreeable banquet choices, snails withdraw into their shells and become dormant. "At the first hint of frost our snail feels the approach of a resistless lassitude," wrote Ernest Ingersoll in his 1879 essay, titled "In a Snailery." "Creeping under some moldering log or half-buried bowlder [sic], it attaches itself, aperture upward, by exuding a little glue." They seal up the shell's opening with a layer of mucus, which dries into taut parchment. If it is cold enough, the snail will retreat farther inward and stretch another barrier across the shell, creating an insulating layer of air. It will then spend the winter, in Ingersoll's words, "snugly coiled in the deepest recesses of his domicile." By putting their already slow life on pause in this manner, garden snails can survive temperatures down to 23°F. Scotland's snails routinely hibernate for seven months of the year. And in some cases, dormancy can last several years. Snails of other species have revived after an interlude encased in a block of ice. If I didn't tune my snail's living conditions to its preferences, its patience would certainly outlast mine.

Sleeping Travelers

Snails nearly drove Charles Darwin mad. In a letter to a friend, the botanist Joseph Hooker, Darwin wrote, "I have for [the] last 15 months been tormented & haunted by land mollusca." Darwin's problem was that snails had been found on every island that naturalists had searched, and he could not conceive of a means by which snails could have leaped over the ocean to reach them all. This seemed a victory for the creationist idea that God had distributed the animals. If he could not explain how snails had reached the islands, it was a sign that some element of Darwin's reasoning was wrong.

The solution lay in a snail's ability to go dormant. Dormancy could, paradoxically, allow snails to move across great distances. After much frustration and anxiety, Darwin tried dropping dormant snails into seawater for varying periods of time. When one of these snails revived, Darwin wrote, it "quite astonished & delighted me. I feel as if a thousand pound weight was taken off my back." A snail hibernating in the crevice of a branch could easily float six hundred miles in an ocean current, he calculated.

Darwin later realized that snails could also leap the oceans by sticking themselves to migrating birds. Scientists have confirmed that snails do hitch rides in this way, attaching themselves to bird feathers, mammal hairs, and insect exoskeletons: "a tiny snail has been known to catch a ride on the leg of a bee," Bailey wrote.

Many species of snails are minuscule. One day, while watering the maidenhair fern on my desk, I noticed a little shell. It was empty, and barely big enough to cover the "o" on the back of a penny. I'd nearly passed it over as a speck of dirt, but some part of my brain registered its order and symmetry. It was only when I transferred it to a white sheet of paper (carefully—it was too small to pick up with a thumb and forefinger) that it revealed itself to me.

It must have lived in the fern. Perhaps there were others.

What did it eat? And how had it met its end? Was it the victim
of some tiny predator? I started imagining the food web that
must exist in the pot at my elbow. *What else have I been missing,* I wondered, *because I've never before taken the time to
examine the dust?*

Mollusk Moonwalk

After spending two weeks cemented to the glass, my snail moved
to the bottom of the jar. I picked it up, thinking that it must have
fallen because it had finally dried up. It was as light as a frozen
pea in my fingers. I rolled it over. The shell opening had changed
shape, and now looked more triangular than oval. Then I saw
why: A foot was slowly emerging from the shell. Still worried
that the snail might be desiccated, I quickly dipped it in water.
Immediately the head emerged and the horns peeped out. I positioned it next to the camellia blossom. It steamed off my thumb
and onto the petals while I waited (and waited).

There's something transfixing about snail locomotion. They
move without any visible sign of movement, like a wakeless ship
ghosting over the water. It was miraculous to watch, as if I'd
suddenly gained the ability to see plants grow or leaves change
color.

A snail moves by flexing its foot, sending a series of tiny
waves through the surface. These ripples briefly turn the mucus
it secretes from a solid to a liquid, allowing it to glide. Snails are
like cross-country skiers, but instead of pushing off with one ski
as they glide on the other, they do it all on one ski, pushing with
part of the surface and gliding on the rest.

A snail will sometimes "gallop," lifting the forward part of its foot and jumping over a bit of ground. A galloping snail leaves a dotted track rather than a continuous trail of slime. There is one species that, when provoked, does a sort of wheelie, rearing up on the back of its foot and speeding off, relatively speaking.

The slime that snails use to walk is called pedal mucus. It is this that allows them to travel up walls and sleep upside down on the underside of leaves. "So tenacious is this exudation that some species can hang in mid-air by spinning out a mucous thread," wrote Ingersoll.

As my snail traversed the petals of the camellia blossom, it waved its antennae expressively. At times they would stretch forward, at others they hung limp. It was easy to infer human feeling in these movements: yearning, excitement, curiosity, disappointment. Josephine, who had crawled up into my lap when she found me watching the reanimated snail, smiled at these antics. The snail's young body was transparent and we could plainly see the dark nerve pathways running from its eye-stalk to form tiny dots in the bulbous tips. When Josephine swept a hand out to touch the tentacle, the snail sensed the oncoming mass and recoiled. Because we could see through the skin, we were able to watch the eyes and their dark connecting cables retracting through the antennae and back into the head. If the antennae are telescopic towers, the eye is the watchman that climbs the tower and can just as quickly retreat.

The snail seemed uninterested in the water and the eggshell that I had set in its path. Surmising that the camellia did not suit its tastes, I offered it a crisp leaf of butter lettuce. The snail's antennae strained toward my offering and it sailed forward with what seemed to be great interest. Through my hand lens I could see its open mouth and an upper row of teeth chomping down on the leaf. It had a cartoonish overbite—the snail was completely lacking in the chin department—that I found endearing. As I peered at it I could hear, faintly but unmistakably, the sound of its thousands of tiny teeth crunching lettuce.

Snails are hermaphrodites. They can fertilize their own eggs, and when they mate they both give and receive sperm. To ensure that its partner will use its sperm, a snail can lance its mate with a hollow "love dart." These barbed harpoons contain an injection of sex hormones, which increases the chance that the harpooner will become a father. The darts are made of calcium carbonate and kept in a special interior sac. Garden snails carry just one dart at a time. They are typically about an inch long and gently curved, with four blades running along the length like a hunting arrowhead.

SLOWING DOWN

My snail fled its jar the night after it revived. I wish it well. I hope it found its way outside, or into the moist soil at the base of a houseplant. Bailey, after eventually growing well, released her snail, along with its progeny.

Most people, I think, are not so fond of snails. As Ingersoll wrote, "Two-thirds of the persons to whom I show the little land and fresh-water mollusks in my snailery either start back with an 'Oh! the horrid things!' which causes me some amusement, or else gaze straight out of the window, saying languidly, 'How interesting!' which hurts my pride."

I can understand. Most people notice snails only when they come to eat their gardens. They are so fundamentally alien from us that they provoke a natural fear of the unknown. But if you have a little patience, this strangeness makes snails wonderful for watching. Reflecting on her relationship with her snail, Bailey told her doctor, "Watching another creature go about its life . . . somehow gave me, the watcher, purpose too. If life mattered to the snail and the snail mattered to me, it meant something in my life mattered, so I kept on."

Meaning is hard to come by if you are a solitary entity. If you have doubts about your own usefulness and purpose, it is all but impossible to answer those doubts while unmoored. When you are able to affix yourself somehow, to bridge the abyss with a relationship with another creature of any sort, it's easier to make the case that there is some way in which the whole of creation matters, that it has, if not a purpose, at least an invigorating vitality. I find satisfaction in hitching myself to the universe as an observer of this energy, manifest in wonderful complexity. I matter, because it matters. Human self-awareness allows us to question our purpose. But that self-awareness also allows us to watch ourselves experiencing wonder, curiosity, and the delight of discovery, and therefore to value those things. Our role may be fulfilled, perhaps, simply by paying close attention. Maybe that's the meaning.

CONCLUSION

THE SPECIES THAT I'VE WRITTEN about here are, at best, invisible, and at worst, reviled. We honor least the nature that is closest to us. As Courtney Humphries put it in *Superdove,* "We create and destroy habitat, we shape genomes, we aid the world-wide movement of other species. And yet we seem disappointed and horrified when those plants and animals respond by adapting to our changes and thriving in them."

Because they are associated with human disruption, the organisms that spring up from our footprints look like corruptions of nature. But I've come to see it the other way around: These species represent nature at its most vital and creative.

Nature never misses an opportunity to exploit a catastrophe. When humans bulldoze and pave, nature sends in a vanguard of species that can tough it out in the new environment. These invasive species are not nature's destroyers, but rather its creators. They begin setting up food webs, they evolve and diverge into new species. Because humans purposefully import exotic plants—along with the insects, seeds, and microbes we accidentally bring in from around the world—cities are remarkable centers of biodiversity. These creatures crossbreed, hybridize, eat one another, form cooperative relationships, and evolve. And so, at a time when thousands of species are at risk of extinction because of our destruction of wilderness, new species are springing up in the new habitats we have created. And it's not just one or two new species: The conservation biologist Chris Thomas, who studies the emergence of species in human-dominated areas, has estimated the increase in plant species over the last 150 years is just about equal to the extinction rate for mammals.

We tend to think of nature and civilization as being irreconcilably opposed: Civilization's gain is nature's loss. But in fact, cities have become prime habitat for speciation, hybridization, and, in short, rebirth. Certainly, civilization has upended the status quo in nature, but it is also proving to be a vehicle for a natural renaissance.

This doesn't mean that we should stop worrying about extinctions and the environment. Earth as a whole is going to be fine, but the Sumatran tiger is not going to be fine. And many humans are not going to be fine. By altering the climate, we are making the world less hospitable to humanity too, and the poorest among us have already begun to suffer.

As more people have moved to cities, a romantic mode of

thinking about nature has grown more dominant. If you ask city dwellers if they want to preserve biodiversity, the vast majority say yes, but that's very different from truly valuing the natural world. It's all very well to romanticize nature when it is far away, but the real test comes when nature asserts itself in our lives. Then we remember that nature is not only awe-inspiring, but also annoying, capricious, deadly. We are alienated from the natural world, and so we long for it—or at least for an Edenic version of it that never existed. However, if we can see the urban wilderness all around us, I think we will engage with nature more realistically. Instead of glorifying only untouched wilderness, we might build an environmental ethic that allows humans and nature to live together, an ethic that—instead of telling us to stop spoiling nature—would tell us how to use nature to support ourselves.

We might begin to honor and respect the people who deal directly with the natural world—the farmers, the miners, the loggers—who make our lives possible. City dwellers often denounce these people for defiling nature while simultaneously demanding the raw materials they provide. If we had a more realistic sense of the give-and-take necessary for living with nature, we might begin to value their hands-on experience. We might see that we need their practical knowledge to guide us to true sustainability.

How do we reach that place where we might use nature carefully, mindfully, to meet the needs of humanity? The first step is to stop thinking of nature as something far away that we must save from someone else and start seeing it all around us. The first step is to open our eyes to the existence of nature in our daily lives.

All this talk of accepting the reality of nature might sound as if I'm arguing for disenchantment. My purpose is precisely the opposite: The point of this book is re-enchantment. Instead of glorifying some distant and mythologized version of nature, I argue for the magic of the real.

It only makes sense that my daughter inspired this project: It is clear to a child that we live in a world full of magic. As we grow older, tedium and laziness erode this sense of wonder. We get used to things. We stop seeing them.

Rachel Carson wrote that she wished for all children "a sense of wonder so indestructible that it would last throughout life, as an unfailing antidote against the boredom and disenchantments of later years." Parents who are able to nurture that sense of wonder give their children a great gift. And for those of us who feel it slipping away in ourselves, it's not too late. The cure is to simply watch the natural world closely and patiently until your eyes burn through the scrim hung by your expectations and you catch sight of something wholly unexpected.

This act of wizardry, of re-enchantment, takes work. You can't do it all the time. It's simply not possible to always see the world fresh and in full, like a child, while also making money, paying bills on time, and taking care of a family. There's a reason my brain had created a shorthand for noting and dismissing "generic" trees: They are not important in meeting my immediate needs, are not a threat, and are not going to make the rent more affordable. It would be hard to function if like a two-year-old I became so transfixed by a seedpod that I forget to go to work.

But doing this work and *occasionally* acting like a two-year-old pays dividends of awe and pleasure. It doesn't take very much time to notice that you live within nature: It can happen while you're waiting for the bus in the morning, or eating lunch, or walking home in the evening. Wonder doesn't come from outside after driving somewhere spectacular, it comes from within: It's a union of the natural world and the mind prepared to receive it.

"A person with a clear heart and open mind can experience the wilderness anywhere on earth. It is a quality of one's own consciousness," the poet Gary Snyder said. "The planet is a wild place and always will be."

If we come to love nature not only when it is rare and beautiful, but also when it is commonplace and even annoying, I believe it will heal the great wound of our species: our self-imposed isolation from the rest of life, our loneliness for nature. We might remember that we are no different from our surroundings, that the trees and birds are as much our neighbors as other humans. We might remember that before the land belonged to us, we belonged to it. We could belong again.

ENDNOTE

IN THE TIME IT'S TAKEN me to write this book, its inspiration—
Josephine—has grown from a chubby arrangement of dimples
and curiosity into a slender girl with adamant opinions, a distinct sense of fashion, and an overriding conviction that she is
right about everything. As she developed her earliest interests, it
seemed that she was not cut out to obsess over weeds and squirrels like her father. I could live with that. After all, my definition
of the natural world leaves out a lot. For example, I've
neglected the microscopic in this book; what about gut bacte-
ria, and houseplant mycelium, and the mites that live on our
faces? And why stop at biology? What about the geological for-
mations beneath our feet, the movements of water and weather
all around us? What about the properties of starlight? And
aren't our bodies part of the natural world? What about the

chemistry of wonder, the inspiration and exhalation of breath? And is there any reason to exclude the art, music, and religious traditions humans have created to make sense of all this? It's hard to prove that anything, no matter how lowbrow or arcane, is *not* the study of nature.

So when Josephine entered a girly phase I wasn't *too* disappointed. But I was a little disappointed. Every once in a while she'd see me examining something and ask me what I was looking at. She was interested; it's just that she was a lot more interested in dancing like a ballerina and dressing like a princess. When I suggested that she might want to be a scientist instead, she would tell me that that was not for girls.

Then one morning as we set out on our walk to daycare, Josephine spotted a line of ants crawling across our driveway. They stood out in the low-angle light, casting shadows that moved with them. Josephine was pleased with herself for discovering the ants. Then she asked me if they sleep at night. I had no clue.

"I don't know," I said. "But I can ask my friend. She's a bug scientist." I was talking about ant scientist Eleanor Spicer Rice.

The word "she" paired with "bug scientist" seemed to strike Josephine.

"Your friend the bug scientist is a girl?" She pondered silently. A few minutes later she twisted around in her stroller and announced: "I changed my idea, Papa. I don't want to be a ballerina. Can I be a bug scientist?"

"You can be anything you want," I told her as evenly as I could manage. My heart did a secret victory dance.

This is probably just another phase, but it's one with some

staying power. She borrows my hand lens to peer at spiders, stops every day on the way out the back door to check on the paper wasps' nest under the railing, and eagerly calls me over to identify insects she's found. The other day she pointed out a big snail making its way over a slender bridge of grass stems. She swept a hand over it and crowed with delight as it retracted its horns.

"This is a good adventure for a bug scientist," she exclaimed.

I'll admit to feeling immoderately pleased. I fear I will always be a poor and bumbling naturalist, forever in the awkward early stages of a relationship with nature. But perhaps there's hope for the next generation.

ACKNOWLEDGMENTS

THIS BOOK IS LARGELY A COLLAGE: I searched out the brightest bits from other people's hordes of knowledge, pilfered them, and pasted them here. I'm indebted to those who provided material for the pilfering. Steve Barley indulged me by engaging in an earnest correspondence about videos of squirrels running obstacle courses. Philip Stark took me foraging, and has become a wise counselor on topics ranging beyond weeds. Charlie Walcott and Daniel Haag-Wackernagle directed my search on pigeons, and Haag-Wackernagle even sent me a copy of his beautifully illustrated book, all the way from Switzerland, complete with a translation from the German. Michael Steele and Mikel Delgado gave me with more charming squirrel facts than I could use. Nathan Talbot provided the mystery that gave me a reason to listen to birds, and Mike Nelson was there to offer pragmatic guidance when birdsong became overwhelming. I am lucky to live in the same place as the world authority on turkey vultures, John Long, a busy man who doesn't care much for e-mail or telephone interviews, but who may be lured into conversation with good beer. John Marzluff helped me understand the dynamics of birds around cities, and Kaeli Swift spend several hours patiently debunking my assumptions about crow behavior, and nudging me toward much more interesting facts. Josh Klein was wonderfully insightful, and tremendous fun to boot. I owe special thanks to Eleanor Spicer Rice, who probably spent more time than any other expert in helping me understand my environment. To all the people who shared their stories with me, I offer my sincere thanks, especially those who reviewed the chapters and corrected mistakes. Any errors that remain are mine alone.

I'm also grateful to all the authors and scientists who wrote the books I drew from. They are noted in the text and in the bibliography. I hope readers seek them out. To casual readers, I especially recommend *Superdove* and *The Sound of a Wild Snail Eating*. So good!

My agent Nicole Tourtelot nurtured this book from conception to completion. My editor Alex Postman launched the project, and when she moved on to other things, Mollie Thomas gracefully stepped in to bring it home. There are several more people at Rodale whose names I don't know, who understood the book deeply and found exactly the right way to express its tenor in design, and transform it into a physical object. I appreciate all the magic that this team has worked.

Many thanks to Jennifer Kahn for spending all those Tuesdays in the teahouse with me, writing and talking about writing. To Daniel Herman, a tip of the hat for introducing me to Vast Aire.

My colleagues at *Grist* were an unstinting source of good humor and good company. Special thanks to the editorial team: Brentin Mock, Greg Hanscom, Ben Adler, Eve Andrews, Darby Smith, Ted Alvarez, Scott Rosenberg, Amelia Urry, Daniel Penner, Lisa Hymas, Andrew Simon, Katie Herzog, Amelia Bates, Mignon Khargie, and Heather Smith.

My family deserves special credit for this book. Josephine inspired the whole thing of course, and kept me honest by being a mostly uncooperative collaborator. That is, she was like herself rather than the character who would have fit more easily, but also more tritely, into these pages. I don't know if I can make the case that her little sister, Jules, assisted in this project as there are several hundred hours of lost sleep weighing the scales in the other direction. But I suppose a good lawyer would point out that she could have woken up *more* in the middle of the night, and that, all things considered, she did everything that could be reasonably asked of a baby. I'm grateful for that, and for her enthusiastic embrace of the world's minutiae. My greatest partner was my wife, Beth, who made this all possible in a thousand tiny, and several large, ways.

BIBLIOGRAPHY

INTRODUCTION

Hartop, Emily A., Brian V. Brown, and R. Henry L. Disney. "Opportunity in Our Ignorance: Urban Biodiversity Study Reveals 30 New Species and One New Nearctic Record for Megaselia (Diptera: Phoridae) in Los Angeles (California, USA)." *Zootaxa* 3941, no. 4 (April 2, 2015): 451–84. doi:10.11646/zootaxa.3941.4.1.

Stegner, Wallace, and T. H. Watkins. *Where the Bluebird Sings to the Lemonade Springs: Living and Writing in the West.* Reprint ed. New York: Modern Library, 2002.

Sullivan, Michael. *The Trees of San Francisco.* San Francisco: Pomegranate Communications, 2004.

On Annie Dillard:

Saverin, Diana. "The Thoreau of the Suburbs." *The Atlantic,* February 5, 2015.

PIGEON

I drew primarily from:

Blechman, Andrew D. *Pigeons: The Fascinating Saga of the World's Most Revered and Reviled Bird.* New York: Grove Press, 2007.

Humphries, Courtney. *Superdove.* HarperCollins e-books, 2009.

Johnston, Richard F., and Marián Janiga. *Feral Pigeons.* New York: Oxford University Press, 1995.

I also relied on:

Haag-Wackernagel, Daniel. "Culture History of the Pigeon— Kulturgeschichte Der Taube." Accessed August 17, 2015. https://anatomie.unibas.ch/IntegrativeBiology/haag/Culture-History -Pigeon/feral-pigeon-haag.html.

———. *Die Taube: Vom heiligen Vogel der Liebesgöttin zur Strassentaube.* Basel: Schwabe, 1998.

On passenger pigeons:

Price, Jennifer. *Flight Maps: Adventures with Nature in Modern America.* New York: Basic Books, 1999.

On Cher Ami:

Lane, Rose Wilder. "A Bit of Gray in a Blue Sky: The Beautiful Story of the Bird That Saved the Lost Battalion." *Ladies' Home Journal* 36, no. 8 (1919).

On pigeon's mediating human relationships:

Jerolmack, Colin. *The Global Pigeon.* Fieldwork Encounters and Discoveries Series. Chicago: University of Chicago Press, 2013.

On pigeons as messengers for China's military:

Jiang, Chengcheng. "China's Most Secret Weapon: The Messenger Pigeon." *Time.* Accessed August 17, 2015. http://content.time.com /time/world/article/0,8599,2049569,00.html.

See also:

Abs, Michael, ed. *Physiology and Behaviour of the Pigeon.* London; New York: Academic Press, 1983.

Gibbs, David, Eustace Barnes, and John Cox. *Pigeons and Doves: A Guide to the Pigeons and Doves of the World.* New Haven, CT: Yale University Press, 2001.

Goodwin, Derek. *Pigeons and Doves of the World.* 3rd ed. [London]: British Museum (Natural History); Ithaca, NY: Comstock Pub. Associates, 1983.

WEEDS

I drew primarily from:

Gibbons, Euell. *Stalking the Wild Asparagus.* Woodstock, VT: Alan C. Hood & Company, 1962.

Lerner, Rebecca. *Dandelion Hunter: Foraging the Urban Wilderness.* Guilford, CT: Lyons Press, 2013.

Wong, Tama Matsuoka, Eddy Leroux, and Daniel Boulud. *Foraged Flavor: Finding Fabulous Ingredients in Your Backyard or Farmer's Market, with 88 Recipes.* New York: Clarkson Potter, 2012.

On the (potentially) positive effects of plant toxins:

Velasquez-Manoff, M. "Fruits and Vegetables Are Trying to Kill You," *Nautilus*, no. 15 (July 3, 2014), http://nautil.us/issue/15/turbulence /fruits-and-vegetables-are-trying-to-kill-you.

On the relationship between poverty and obesity:

Drewnowski, Adam, and S. E. Specter. "Poverty and Obesity: The Role of Energy Density and Energy Costs." *The American Journal of Clinical Nutrition* 79, no. 1 (January 1, 2004): 6–16.

These guidebooks also proved useful:

Thayer, Samuel. *Nature's Garden: A Guide to Identifying, Harvesting, and Preparing Edible Wild Plants.* Birchwood, WI: Forager's Harvest Press, 2010.

Tredici, Peter Del, and Steward T. A. Pickett. *Wild Urban Plants of the Northeast: A Field Guide.* Ithaca, NY: Comstock Publishing Associates, 2010.

Zachos, Ellen. *Backyard Foraging: 65 Familiar Plants You Didn't Know You Could Eat.* North Adams, MA: Storey Publishing, 2013.

SQUIRREL

I drew primarily from:

Steele, Michael A., and John L. Koprowski. *North American Tree Squirrels.* Washington, DC: Smithsonian Books, 2003.

On the campaign to bring squirrels to cities:

Benson, Etienne. "The Urbanization of the Eastern Gray Squirrel in the United States." *Journal of American History* 100, no. 3 (December 1, 2013): 691–710. doi:10.1093/jahist/jat353.

On Seton and Roosevelt:

Seton, Ernest Thompson. *Animal Heroes*, 2000. http://www.gutenberg .org/ebooks/2284.

———. *Wild Animals I Have Known*, 2002. http://www.gutenberg.org /ebooks/3031.

Watts, Sarah. *Rough Rider in the White House: Theodore Roosevelt and the Politics of Desire.* Chicago: University of Chicago Press, 2006.

See also:

Adler, Bill, Jr. *Outwitting Squirrels: 101 Cunning Stratagems to Reduce Dramatically the Egregious Misappropriation of Seed from Your Birdfeeder by Squirrels.* 2nd ed. Chicago: Chicago Review Press, 1996.

Appleman, Philip. "Darwin's Bestiary." Accessed August 17, 2015. http://www.poetryfoundation.org/poem/175912.

Barkalow, Frederick Schenck. *The World of the Gray Squirrel.* Philadelphia: Lippincott Williams & Wilkins, 1973.

Thorington, Richard, Jr., and Katie E. Ferrell. *Squirrels: The Animal Answer Guide.* Baltimore: Johns Hopkins University Press, 2006.

BIRD LANGUAGE

I drew primarily from:

Young, Jon. *What the Robin Knows: How Birds Reveal the Secrets of the Natural World.* Boston: Houghton Mifflin Harcourt, 2012.

See also:

Krause, Bernie. *The Great Animal Orchestra: Finding the Origins of Music in the World's Wild Places.* New York: Little, Brown and Company, 2012.

Walker, Matt. "Noise Pollution Threatens Animals." *BBC*, October 14, 2009, Earth News sec. http://news.bbc.co.uk/earth/hi/earth_news/newsid_8305000/8305320.stm.

GINKGO

I drew primarily from:

Crane, Peter. *Ginkgo: The Tree That Time Forgot.* New Haven, CT: Yale University Press, 2013.

On ginkgo's missing seed distributors:

Del Tredici, Peter. "Ginkgos and Multituberculates: Evolutionary Interactions in the Tertiary." *Biosystems* 22, no. 4 (1989): 327–39. doi:10.1016/0303-2647(89)90054-3.

———. "The Phenology of Sexual Reproduction in Ginkgo Biloba: Ecological and Evolutionary Implications." *Botanical Review* 73, no. 4 (October 1, 2007): 267–78. doi:10.1663/0006-8101(2007)73[267:TPOSRI]2.0.CO;2.

On Oliver Sacks:

Sacks, Oliver W. *The Island of the Colorblind and Cycad Island.* New York: Alfred A. Knopf, 1997.

See also:

Hugo, Nancy R., and Robert Llewellyn. *Seeing Trees: Discover the Extraordinary Secrets of Everyday Trees.* Portland, OR: Timber Press, 2011.

Phillips, Carolyn. *All Under Heaven: Recipes from the 35 Cuisines of China.* Berkeley, CA: Ten Speed Press, 2016.

Plotnik, Arthur. *The Urban Tree Book: An Uncommon Field Guide for City and Town.* New York: Three Rivers Press, 2000.

TURKEY VULTURE

Most of what has been written about turkey vultures is in scientific journals, and there's not a huge amount of that. I leaned heavily on Douglas Long.

On the extinct reratorns:

Campbell, Kenneth E., Jr., and Eduardo P. Tonni. "Size and Locomotion in Teratorns (Aves: Teratornithidae)." *Auk* 100, no. 2 (April 1, 1983): 390–403.

Chatterjee, Sankar, R. Jack Templin, and Kenneth E. Campbell. "The Aerodynamics of Argentavis, the World's Largest Flying Bird from the Miocene of Argentina." *Proceedings of the National Academy of Sciences* 104, no. 30 (July 24, 2007): 12398–403. doi:10.1073 /pnas.0702040104.

"Extinct Teratorn Fact Sheet." Accessed August 17, 2015. http://library .sandiegozoo.org/factsheets/_extinct/teratorn/teratorn. htm#distribution.

See also:

Bertelsen, Martin Leonhard. "Vultures Evolved an Extreme Gut to Cope with Disgusting Dietary Habits," November 25, 2014. http://geogenetics .ku.dk/latest-news/vultures/.

Rajchard, J. "Exogenous Chemical Substances in Bird Perception: A Review." *Veterinari Medicina* 53, no. 8 (2008): 412–19.

"Turkey Vulture." Accessed August 17, 2015. http://128.84 .12.93/guidebeta/lifehistory.aspx/?spp=Turkey_Vulture.

ANT

I drew primarily from:

Gordon, Deborah. *Ant Encounters: Interaction Networks and Colony Behavior.* Princeton, NJ: Princeton University Press, 2010.

Moffett, Mark W. *Adventures among Ants: A Global Safari with a Cast of Trillions.* Berkeley, CA: University of California Press, 2010.

Wilson, Edward O., and Burt Hölldobler. *Journey to the Ants: A Story of Scientific Exploration.* Cambridge, MA: Belknap Press, 1994.

On slave-making ants:

Topoff, Howard. "Slave-making queens," *Scientific American,* 281, no. 5 (November 1999): 84–90.

Ant water-harvesting:

Moffett, Mark W. "An Indian Ant's Novel Method for Obtaining Water." *National Geographic Research* 1, no. 1 (1985): 146–49.

On ant self-sacrifice:

Tofilski, Adam, and Margaret Couvillon. "Preemptive Defensive Self-Sacrifice by Ant Workers." *American Naturalist* 175, no. 5 (2008): E239–43. doi:10.1086/591688.

On honeybees collecting insect honeydew:

Santas, Loukas A. "Insects Producing Honeydew Exploited by Bees in Greece." *Apidologie* 14, no. 2 (1983): 93–103. doi:10.1051/apido:19830204.

On Argentine ants, and their impact:

Brattstrom, Bayard H. "Distribution of the Coast Horned Lizard, Phrynosoma Coronatum, in Southern California." *Bulletin, Southern California Academy of Sciences* 112, no. 3 (December 1, 2013): 206–16 doi:10.3160/0038-3872-112.3.206.

Brightwell, R. J., P. E. Labadie, and J. Silverman. "Northward Expansion of the Invasive Linepithema Humile (Hymenoptera: Formicidae) in the Eastern United States Is Constrained by Winter Soil Temperatures." *Environmental Entomology* 39, no. 5 (October 2010): 1659–65. doi:10.1603/EN09345.

Keller, Laurent, and Denis Fournier. "Lack of Inbreeding Avoidance in the Argentine Ant Linepithema Humile." *Behavioral Ecology* 13, no. 1 (January 1, 2002): 28–31. doi:10.1093/beheco/13.1.28.

Krieger, M. J., and L. Keller. "Mating Frequency and Genetic Structure of the Argentine Ant Linepithema Humile." *Molecular Ecology* 9, no. 2 (February 2000): 119–26.

On the destructiveness of invasive species:

Cooling, Meghan, Stephen Hartley, Dalice A. Sim, and Philip J. Lester. "The Widespread Collapse of an Invasive Species: Argentine Ants (*Linepithema Humile*) in New Zealand." *Biology Letters* 8, no. 3 (June 23, 2012): 430–33. doi:10.1098/rsbl.2011.1014.

Pearce, Fred. *The New Wild: Why Invasive Species Will Be Nature's Salvation.* Boston: Beacon Press, 2015.

Suarez, Andrew V., Jon Q. Richmond, and Ted J. Case. "Prey Selection in Horned Lizards Following the Invasion of Argentine Ants in Southern California." *Ecological Applications* 10, no. 3 (June 1, 2000): 711–25. doi:10.1890/1051-0761(2000)010[0711:PSIHLF]2.0.CO;2.

CROW

I drew primarily from:

Haupt, Lyanda Lynn. *Crow Planet: Essential Wisdom from the Urban Wilderness.* New York: Little, Brown and Company, 2009.

Marzluff, John, and Tony Angell. *Gifts of the Crow: How Perception, Emotion, and Thought Allow Smart Birds to Behave Like Humans.* New York: Atria Books, 2012.

On DDT and raptors:

Preston, Charles R. *Red-Tailed Hawk.* Mechanicsburg, PA: Stackpole Books, 2000.

On animal play:

Sharpe, Lynda. "So You Think You Know Why Animals Play . . . " *ScientificAmerican.com* (guest blog), May 17, 2011. http://blogs .scientificamerican.com/guest-blog/so-you-think-you-know-why -animals-play/.

On bird diversity in urban areas:

DeBare, Ilana. "Counting Crows: Why Are There so Many in Berkeley?" *Berkeleyside.* Accessed August 17, 2015. http://www.berkeleyside .com/2014/03/28/counting-crows-why-are-there-so-many-in -berkeley/.

Marzluff, John M. *Welcome to Subirdia.* New Haven, CT: Yale University Press, 2014.

Shultz, Allison J., Morgan W. Tingley, and Rauri C. K. Bowie. "A Century of Avian Community Turnover in an Urban Green Space in Northern California." *Condor* 114, no. 2 (May 1, 2012): 258–67. doi:10.1525/cond.2012.110029.

US EPA, Office of Research and Development. "EPA's Report on the Environment." Reports & Assessments. Accessed August 17, 2015. http://cfpub.epa.gov/roe/indicator.cfm?i=83#1.

SNAIL

I drew primarily from:

Bailey, Elisabeth Tova. *The Sound of a Wild Snail Eating.* Chapel Hill, NC: Algonquin Books, 2010.

See also:

"Darwin Correspondence Project » Letter: 2018." Accessed August 17, 2015. https://www.darwinproject.ac.uk/letter/entry-2018.

Ingersoll, Ernest. "'In a Snailery,' *Scribner's Monthly, The Century Magazine,* April 1879, 796–802." *UNZ.org.* Accessed August 17, 2015. http://www.unz.org/Pub/Century-1879apr-00796.

Weir, James. *The Dawn of Reason: Or, Mental Traits in the Lower Animals.* New York; London: Macmillan, 1899.

CONCLUSION

Carson, Rachel, and Nick Kelsh. *The Sense of Wonder.* New York: HarperCollins, 1998.

Cronon, William. "The Trouble with Wilderness: Or, Getting Back to the Wrong Nature." *Environmental History* 1, no. 1 (January 1996): 7. doi:10.2307/3985059.

Marris, Emma. *The Rambunctious Garden: Saving Nature in a Post-Wild World.* Reprint ed. New York: Bloomsbury USA, 2013.

Thomas, Chris D. "Rapid Acceleration of Plant Speciation during the Anthropocene." *Trends in Ecology & Evolution* 30, no. 8 (January 8, 2015): 448–55. doi:10.1016/j.tree.2015.05.009.

INDEX